Shamanism & the Spirit Mate

Experiencing the Ecstasy of the Celestial Lover

Shamanism & the Spirit Mate

Experiencing the Ecstasy of the Celestial Lover

Shana Robinson & Dana Robinson

EWH Press

MICHIGAN, 2012

Published by EWH Press
PO Box 537
Leslie, MI 49251
www.ewhpress.com

ISBN 978-0-9834438-7-2
EWH Press first printing, November 2012

Cover and book design by Terrie MacNicol
Cover art by Shana Robinson
Edited by Jeff Stoner

Printed in the United States of America

To lovers and seekers everywhere...

In honor of the spirits...

Contents

Acknowledgments

It has been our blessing to have wise teachers over the years. But for their ground-breaking work and their belief in us, we would not be writing or experiencing life in the enriched way that we do. We extend our gratitude to Michael and Sandra Harner, not only for their scholarship and hard work, but also for the kindness they share with us. *Grazie, Godfather!* Thank you to Rudy Bauer, who always encouraged us, and helped us to "hold the field." And to Harry Dillingham, bless you wherever you roam; there would be less humor and joy in study if it weren't for you.

For those patient people who held our hands during the production of this work, you have our deepest gratitude. You helped us breathe through the messy bits in the birth of this project—thank you Jeff and Terrie at Earth Wisdom Harmonics Press! And thank you Karen—diligent reader in spite of challenges with childcare, cancelled flights, and power loss.

Our students and our relationship to the spirits are gifts that we hold sacred and continue to marvel at. Their trust in us and their continual help feed us quite literally, and bring us joy in learning and joy in service. Thank you one and all!

—Shana

And to Jenny and Denise; Benita, Alicia and Diona—thank you for all the things that you knowingly gave to me and all the things you don't know that you gave to me. For Janis and all our friends in low places, thanks as plentiful as the hoodoos. Thanks for camp, Mom, and for that special boxed set of weird books for Christmas.

For you, T. Silverwolf, I am grateful for your ever-present voice in my ear. Without your help, this would not be. And to you, too, King D, the poetry is yours. And, Dana, what can I say? Words will never capture the path I am blessed to share with you.

—Dana

Thanks to those actors who inspired us and gave us glimpses of other worlds through their work on the silver screen and the small screen. Thanks Anne, George, Cary and so many others.

A.H., through you I experienced a new and deeper ecstasy that changed me. Thank you. Shana, the gods gave me the most precious gift when you came into my life. You make all the difference. Thank you.

Preface

In all pursuits of knowledge, vision is limited by obstacles both seen and unseen. In our work with the Spirit Mate, we have only seen as far as the next horizon with imperfect vision. It is with this understanding that we submit this work to the reader, knowing that another trek or another explorer will eventually come along and expand the territory we've traveled, adding to this body of work.

We hope that this adventure serves you, dear reader, in some way. We are deeply grateful for all our teachers and students who contributed to this material and our understanding of the Spirit Mate phenomenon. Some of our conclusions are not strictly shamanic. We acknowledge that, and we continue to work to embrace the mysteries as they present themselves to us.

Spirit Mate Principles

1. Two poles at play in the Spirit Mate relationship are: masculine-feminine and human-divine.
2. These poles sexualize and spiritualize the relationship and are the source of the empowerment encapsulated by the relationship.
3. The identity of the Spirit Mate is in most cases represented by a cross-gendered spirit—that is, a being from non-ordinary reality, sometimes known as a god or goddess, that appears to the human partner in the opposite sex.
4. The Spirit Mate can shape-shift, depending on the lesson of the moment. The form of the Spirit Mate can be anything from an object to an animal—wrathful or peaceful.
5. The role of this spirit can be, but is not limited to, that of companion, teacher, guide, angel, inspirer, muse, lover, spouse and consort.
6. Through the relationship with the Spirit Mate there is a potential for the transformation of the human partner. This includes opening to greater personal authenticity and enriched creativity, which further includes a greater capacity to be of service to others.
7. The Spirit Mate is not all knowing, but rather all caring (compassionate).
8. The Spirit Mate may be encountered in an altered state of consciousness—the shamanic journey, a dream, meditation or reverie—and can also manifest in Ordinary Reality.
9. The relationship one has with a Spirit Mate may culminate in a marriage. This marriage represents a spiritual commitment to live fully in authenticity and service. It is a call and a commitment to a higher order of being.
10. The true goal of work with a Spirit Mate is that of the mystic seeking union with the divine.

Introduction

Do not blame Love for the agony it brings;
Love is the King of all paths,
And the heart not wild with longing
Is already dead, already a burial ground.

— Kabir[1]

Relationships punctuate human existence. For most of our lives it is the acquisition of, dissatisfaction with or loss of relationship that colors our moods, our actions, our conversations. We constantly strive to look right, have the right stuff and go to the right places so that we can build relationships on a professional or personal level. Who we are is defined by the terms of relationship: mother, father, lover, 'ex', boss, employee, student, teacher. Yet, even with the vast variety of relationships available to us, there is an overwhelming loneliness that lurks within.[2] It is as if the more we endeavor to connect, link up and network, the deeper the gap between ourselves and the satisfaction of vague, ill-defined longing.[3] We are looking for something, as in a dream, and everywhere we seek it, it eludes us.

This longing has been with us from the instant we became self-aware. For if there is an 'I', there is the 'not I' or 'other'. And in discovering that there is a distinction between the two, a sense of separation from all that is arises. It seeps into our being like a slowly enveloping fog and insinuates the desire to unify, to be a part of a greater whole, to become whole, to fill a hole, prodding us to seek fulfillment.

As the song goes, we look for love in all the wrong places. We seek all manner of stuff to fill our void: clothes, electronics, automobiles, huge homes. We think that 'better, more, bigger, nicer' is the magical answer to the call we hear. We believe that the call is on the physical level. In fact, the call is from a place we have denied, a place deeper than the body, broader than the mind. It is from a place that has almost been eliminated from our human experience. The call comes from our soul.

How are we to answer this call? What technicians of the soul can help us to repair the rift, so that we can satisfy the longing and step away from the false answers?

It is through the ecstatic and the mystic that we can discover the way; they have kept the secret hidden in plain view. We must follow their lead, as Theseus followed his clew, in order to escape the labyrinth of delusion that our overly zealous materialism has created. The journey is one of spirit, and there are many paths that lead to the goal. What follows is an exploration of one of these by-ways.

The soul has been defined as that very minimal spiritual essence required for physical life to exist. Without a soul, there is no life. World cultures look at the concept of soul in varying ways. Some see it as a single unit that can be fractured and fragmented through trauma. Others see it not as a singularity but rather as a mosaic of parts, each part responsible for a particular aspect of life. What is understood is that the soul is the spark that brings life—and through it, consciousness—to the physical being. Like the material body and the not-so-material mind, it needs tending and maintenance to operate harmoniously. Without this attention, soul sickness can result, requiring the service of the technician.

The master soul technicians emerged thousands of years ago: the shamans. The shaman is the ecstatic who recognizes that everything is inspirited and possesses intelligence. The shaman functions on behalf of his community to mediate the flow of power, which is defined as energy plus intelligence.[4] The tool of the shaman is the shamanic journey, the voyage of his spirit (awareness) into the cosmic realms of non-ordinary reality[5] that are called Lower, Middle and Upper Worlds. These realms exist outside of our ordinary reality and outside of time. They can be accessed through monotonous percussion or entheogens. The shaman explores their expanse with the aid of helpers he has found there and with whom he has built relationships.

The relationships that the shaman cultivates with the beings of the other worlds, his helping spirits, often lead to what Michael Harner has called 'mystical, ecstatic unions'. These unions inform and enrich the life and work of the shaman as he unfolds the mysteries of the soul and the ways to tend it. From this expanding wisdom, the shaman serves his community through healing practices and lives in the knowledge that humans are not without help and guidance.

Others, too, have found the path of ecstasy leading to the spirit world. All of the religious traditions of the world have at their core a method for approaching the deity, spirit helpers or the primal consciousness. It is even possible to meet with a being we call the Spirit Mate, a significant other in the spirit world, and form a relationship that ultimately answers the soul's longing and fills the emptiness that the material world cannot fill.

There are many implications for the modern human who engages in a Spirit Mate partnership. The mystical union with a spirit can be a lens that sharpens the human's understanding of and practice with love and relationship. Experiences in the non-ordinary landscapes of the Upper or Lower Worlds—landscapes populated with compassionate, helping spirits—provide an opportunity to gain knowledge that can be applied in ordinary, waking reality. This is the way of the shaman, the way of healing based soundly on the principles of love and ethics. Power comes through the presence and tutelage of helping spirits, including the Spirit Mate. Making and maintaining a non-ordinary relationship with the Spirit Mate can promote growth in interpersonal relationships, deepen spiritual connections, assist in healing practices, and promote creativity.

Creativity is not limited to artistic expression. It enables us to include novel approaches to problems and moves us toward our dreams. As Sandra Harner has pointed out, "something is a problem because it cannot be resolved in the usual way."[6] The Spirit Mate relationship is cultivated through the shamanic journey. These voyages to the Spirit Mate and the Spirit Mate's world provide spiritual experiences which, through what Harner calls incubation (time "set apart from a direct attack on the problem"), promote "a revelation of quite unexpected content—an inspiration."[7] The gift of inspiration, knowledge from the shamanic journey, is a highly personalized power. As power, it is composed of energy that can replenish and fulfill the journeyer and provide impetus to act in new, creative ways. As Julia Cameron has noted, our dreams move us toward our divinity.[8]

Dana first introduced the Spirit Mate work to students in 1995. It became a critical part of our Next Step program in 2004. The web that the modern shamanic practitioner navigates in gaining knowledge and working to effectuate healing relies on relationships that cross ordinary and non-ordinary reality, just as it did for indigenous forebears. Allies include Animal Guardian Spirits, Teachers, Nature Beings, Ancestors and, in traditions that span the globe, the Spirit Mate. The shamanic practitioner today, as shamans throughout history, stands in the circle of these beings and mediates all the power embodied therein. This defines the role of the shaman: to be the clear conduit of divine light and healing energy, the fulcrum between the spirit world and the community.

Since the introduction of this material, many of our students have found and worked with a Spirit Mate. Their experiences can be plotted along a spectrum that ranges from an interesting foray into uncharted territory to a dedicated and committed partnership. Just as in the ethnography, the celestial other[9]—as the Spirit Mate is sometimes called—can manifest as a marvelous friend, a strict tutor or an intimate partner on the order of a spouse. We have had the honor to hear many stories of spontaneous interactions that mirror in key ways the reports from divergent cultures. Yet, beyond the shamanic context, the quest for connection with the numinous and the divine is territory open to all. There is richness to be discovered in this search and satisfaction to be found in delving into the depths of one's own soul. Ultimately, it is a sacred pilgrimage that leads to mystical ecstatic union.

Chapter 1

Art as Life

*"The surface of the blolo image becomes
the virtual surface of the otherworld itself."*
— Philip L. Ravenhill[1]

The Baule of the Ivory Coast are known for their fascinating figurative art. Statues of men and women in traditional and modern guise represent beings from the *blolo* or otherworld. What appears upon first glance to be interesting from an artistic standpoint becomes even more intriguing when the deeper meaning is revealed. These statues of the Baule represent the spiritual spouses, the otherworld lovers of ordinary reality men and women who live typical lives yet have sought relief for some problem through personal relationship across the boundary into the spirit world.

Many aspects of Baule psychology are involved in the relationship with the *blolo*. The initial factor that drives one to seek a *blolo bian*, otherworld male mate, or *blolo bla*, otherworld female mate, is typically a reproductive crisis involving sterility, still birth or infant mortality.[2] Sometimes the failure to make a marriage drives a person to seek or acknowledge an otherworld mate.[3] Once the problem—typically a neglected *blolo* mate—has been 'diagnosed' by a diviner, a statue of the mate is commissioned and through ceremony becomes a tangible link to the otherworld and the being that it represents. This is the initiation of an expected cure for the reproductive crisis or inability to make a marriage.[4] In the case of the Baule, the being is a human spirit that embodies for the ordinary reality human those qualities admired and desired in a mate.

The *blolo* figurine encapsulates meaning for the human in several ways. It represents the constancy of the Spirit Mate's presence in the *blolo*. Since there is no time in the world of spirits, the figurine's existence is the essence of timelessness, forever young. It is also a symbol of the profound, private intimacy of the relationship with the otherworld mate. Finally, it is the embodiment of potential in the real world; that is, it is possible for things to be different and better in ordinary life.[5]

But the Baule go beyond simply creating a statue that represents an ideal mate. One night a week is devoted solely to the Spirit Mate. The human sleeps alone, away from the ordinary reality spouse, and through dream incubation meets the Spirit Mate while asleep.[6] The encounter, which is expressly sexual, is relived during daylight hours through reverie (daydream). For the Baule, this time in dream and reverie is spent having sex with the *blolo* mate. The Baule approaches to the world of spirits—reverie and the sleeping dream—are the same methods used in the revelatory and healing traditions of the Greek dream temples of Asklepius,[7] and are evident in the modern work of Robert Moss.

These activities, along with the very public possession of a figurine declaring that a person has a Spirit Mate, have important consequences for an ordinary reality spouse. In the case of a Baule married couple, there are two triangles involved—the woman, her husband and her *blolo bian;* and the man, his wife and his *blolo bla.* A rivalry is created which keeps certain behavior in check.[8] One especially notable function is that a woman maintains her own identity; her husband cannot subsume her, since he is not the only man in her life.[9] The spirit man inhibits the real-world man's tendency to dominate. The real-world husband's competition with the *blolo bian* can protect a woman's fortunes – he competes with the *blolo bian's* image of financial well-being, attempting to keep his wife in the same style as her otherworld mate 'keeps' her.

Another spirit represented in Baule art is the *asiɛ usu*. This is a nature spirit that approaches a human from the bush and is said to 'mount' the individual.[10] This 'mounting' is a form of voluntary possession and the human who accedes to this arrangement becomes clairvoyant.[11] The relationship is formalized in the same way that the relationship with a *blolo* mate is formalized. A sculpture of the supernatural being is commissioned and the figurine is installed. The human, through this relationship, now becomes a trance diviner or *komiɛn,* and uses the power of nature via the *asiɛ usu* to do diagnostic work.

Through the clairvoyant capacity, the *komiɛn* sees that which is hidden and pronounces truths. The *komiɛn* will sometimes perform public dances merged with the *asiɛ usu*. Besides the *komiɛn,* there are other diviners who use the supernatural power of the Earth and Nature to reveal causes.[12] They often use a tool called an *ngoinman,* a cluster of leather cords weighted with symbols, and the mouse oracle to assist him (or her) in reading the web of a patient's life.[13] This is done in the presence of the client's spouse and extended family, and the diviner ultimately arrives at an explanation and solution for the presenting problem. A typical solution is often the recognition of a neglected Spirit Mate who needs appeasement via the commission and ceremonial installment of the *blolo* figurine.[14]

The Baule are an example of humans intentionally seeking an intimate relationship with a being in the spirit world. They acknowledge and cement these relationships through artistic expression and ceremony. The Baule Spirit Mate relationship serves societal functions beyond the apparent need for healing evidenced by reproductive problems and mirrors the complexity of the physical-world spousal relationship.

From the Workshop Journal: #1

When we facilitate the Spirit Mate workshop, we encourage each participant to write about various aspects of relationship. The journaling exercises which follow focus our attention and promote new understandings of the ways in which we connect with our community. Journey exercises are included for those who have had instructions in the shamanic journey and have met a Power Animal and Teacher. Activities are occasionally offered to bring the ideas into physical reality.

We begin our examination of relationships with those in the human kingdom. While the exercise instruction is almost simplistic, it stimulates reminiscence and is an opportunity to confront patterns of relationship-making. Ultimately, the lists you make could include all the people you have ever known and could then be used in a process known to some as recapitulation.[1]

In the world of the shaman, humans engage in a marketplace of the soul in which we give away soul parts and take soul parts, consciously or unconsciously. Conditions of soul loss arising from such exchanges are often treated with soul retrieval or soul restoration.[2] In recognizing behavior contributing to these exchanges and taking responsibility for the dominion and sovereignty over our own soul space, we become more responsible members of our communities and are able to interact with greater authenticity.

— Journal

List as completely as possible all the people you have ever considered to be friends and all of your family members. Notice the ways in which you make distinctions among friends and note who gives you power and who takes it. Now notice the people you take power from and to whom you relinquish power. Pay attention to the subtle differences in these power exchanges.

Journal

How would you describe your relationships with family and friends using words like *energizing, draining, powerful*, and *deflating*? What other descriptors can you think of?

Chapter 2

The World of Myth

"I remember going to Baptist summer camp and being quite shocked. I was a good little Catholic girl and this was not my idea of St. Bernadette, my image of holiness as captured by Jennifer Jones in The Song of Bernadette. The quiet and serene sense of worship and self-sacrifice—cloaked in feminine humility—was replaced by an ecstatic frenzy punctuated by keyboard and drum. I was more than a little scared. This was not the safe ground of St. Joe's, and forced me to rethink a few things. Here were people doing what I thought we all were doing to connect with God, but it was very different. Ah. The seed was planted; there is more than one way to get to the truth of a thing."

— from author's journal, Summer 1978 (SR)

In the last chapter, the Baule and their relationship to the Spirit Mate phenomenon was examined. It might be easy to dismiss the otherworld mate as exotic and unrelated to cultures of the Western world. However, the phenomenon is evident in familiar tales as well—specifically, in the mythology of various Western cultures.

Joseph Campbell was a dynamic man living the life of an ecstatic. People who knew him were moved by his enthusiasm and the energy that swirled around him like a cyclone. His lifelong study of myth prompts us to enter the world of the Spirit Mate via that avenue. Bill Moyers, a friend and interviewer of Campbell, writes about myth as a metaphor that hides the visible world, a metaphor that veils God.[1] Caitlín Matthews likewise reminds us of the original sense of the word *myth*. It is "a saving story that sees past the surface into deeper places of solution, and not in the misapplied sense of a 'fabrication or lie.'"[2] Until we engage in the shamanic journey—which at our own initiative transports us to the lands beyond the visible world—we must rely upon the realm of the myth and the power of dreams to provide a map to the territory of the Spirit Mate.

The world of the ancient Greeks reveals the unseen territory mapped by myth. In grade school, we learned about Zeus, Apollo, Aphrodite and Demeter. Each of these deities had a divine responsibility for the operation of the world. We learned, too, that the Romans had similar gods and goddesses and were able to translate Zeus to Jupiter, Aphrodite to Venus and Demeter to Ceres, reflecting the shift in dominant culture. Names of the gods and goddesses have become second nature to us, infiltrating our language through words like *vulcanize* and *saturnine*, after Vulcan, the smith of the gods, and Saturn, a brooding Titan.

The gods and their adventures provided the Greeks with a framework for understanding the otherwise incomprehensible. Like the humans who sought to understand the workings of the world through them, the gods lived lives full of drama and intrigue. This included marriage to or illicit relationships with the very humans they ruled. The marriage of otherworldly beings to humans is mentioned in the famous *Dialogues of Plato*. While addressing the question of Socrates' belief in divine agencies, Plato expounds on the subject, making it clear that the demigods or spirits are gods. He goes on to explain that "the demigods are the illegitimate sons of gods, whether by the nymphs or any other mothers, of whom they are said to be the sons—what human being will ever believe that there are no gods if they are the sons of gods?"[3] So, according to Plato, intercourse between the gods and humans was entirely within the norm of behavior, and children of such mixed couplings were the result.

A favorite illegitimate son of such a coupling is Heracles, whose father was Zeus and mother, the mortal Alcmene. The high god's wife Hera was not appeased when this son was named to honor her. (Heracles means Glory to Hera.) From the time that Heracles was born of Alcmene, Hera did her best to destroy him. She sent deadly serpents to his cradle when he was an infant; she drove him mad, causing him to murder his own wife and children. His remorse was so great that he sought a way to make amends. This led him to perform the Twelve Labors (considered impossible) and have many other adventures, making him a hero in the eyes of the Greeks. His actions weren't a quest for personal fame, but rather an application of his gifts in the service of others. Eventually, Heracles married a second time and had several children. His happiness was short lived when Hera continued her campaign of revenge through the gift of an alleged magical shirt. The shirt was poisonous and donning it caused Heracles such pain that he had a pyre built and jumped upon it to end his misery. Zeus took pity on him and grabbed him from the pyre, installed him on Mount Olympus, home of the gods, and made him an immortal being.

Although this tale deals with Heracles, it illustrates a shamanic principle: the hero, like the shaman, does not seek to gratify his ego through his action, but rather applies himself in the service of others.[4] Relevant to the Spirit Mate in the drama of Heracles is the coupling of Zeus with a human woman. To have his way with Alcmene, Zeus disguised himself as her husband. Staging a return from war, Zeus celebrated his 'homecoming', and Alcmene conceived a child. Her real husband returned from war a day later, and a shocked Alcmene deduced the truth. She ultimately gave birth to Heracles.

Zeus often resorted to chicanery to express his love for human women. Another example of his clever use of disguise was in his relationship with Leda, the Queen of Sparta. He approached her as a swan and became her lover. In the way of such tales, the Queen produced an egg from the affair and hatched four children—two belonged to Zeus and two to her husband.

Europa, a princess of Tyre, likewise fell victim to the gentle manner of Zeus when he approached her in the form of a white bull. When she became so beguiled by his ways that she sat astride him for a ride, he leapt into the sea and carried her off to Crete. Three sons were produced from this union.

Io, too, was loved by Zeus. Rather than changing his own form to protect himself from Hera, Zeus turned Io into a white cow. Hera discovered the enchantment and tethered the cow under the watchful eye of Argus, a 100-eyed servant. Zeus used Hermes and his lyre to lull the servant to sleep, then lopped off his head. Io escaped, making her way to Egypt where she resumed her human form.

Divine love for humans was not singularly a male prerogative for the Greeks. The goddesses had their dalliances, too. Aphrodite fell in love with the human male Adonis, as did Persephone. Adonis preferred Aphrodite to Persephone, and the jealous Persephone incited Ares, a godly lover of Aphrodite, to do away with Adonis. Turning into a boar, Ares dispatched Adonis to the Underworld, where Persephone reigned as queen. Aphrodite despaired, and Zeus negotiated a compromise in which Adonis, according to the seasons, spent part of his time with Persephone in the Underworld and part of his time with Aphrodite on Earth.

Thetis was a sea-goddess, and very powerful. Zeus loved her but was afraid of the prophecy predicting that a son she bore would be greater than the father. To avoid having a scion of such power competing with him, Zeus demanded that Thetis marry a mortal. Peleus was chosen and guided to Thetis on the seashore. He grabbed her and she struggled against his embrace, employing her talents as a shape-shifter. Although she slipped in and out of many forms, Peleus held her in his embrace and Thetis agreed to marry him.

In addition to the Greeks and Romans, the Norse also had tales of the gods crossing into the human realm. Heimdall, the god who watches over Bifrost—the rainbow bridge between Midgard, or Earth, and Asgard, the world of the gods and goddesses—visited Earth dressed as a human man called Rig. He was entertained by peasant folk, Ai and Edda, and given the meager hospitality they could offer for three nights. As a reward, Heimdall left Edda with a son. Rig continued his journey and found hospitality once again, this time at the home of Afi and Amma, who were better off than Ai and Edda. Amma was also left with a son. A further three days at the grand home of Fathir and Mothir produced yet another son as a gift of gratitude.

The Valkyries of Nordic tradition also had a role as spirit wives. They were the special attendants of Odin, the king of the Aesir, or sky gods, who lived in Asgard. Besides carrying out Odin's wishes, which gave rise to the appellation 'wish-maidens', they were the escorts of fallen heroes on the journey to Valhalla. Meeting the slain hero in his grave, a Valkyrie would arouse him with a kiss and guide him to the Hall of Heroes where he would be Odin's guest. As allies to the living, the Valkyries would teach and aid the warrior, rewarding him after battle with erotic love and acting as spirit wives.[5]

In these classic mythical accounts from various Western cultures, what becomes evident is that the boundary between the world of the gods or spirits and the world of humans is much more permeable than one would think. Mere mortals are touched by the divine in unusual ways and bear the consequences of this interaction in many forms, not the least of which is offspring. But can the human initiate the connection with a god/goddess?

The Celts answer this affirmatively. In one tale, the fairy goddess Aine was sitting on the bank of the river Camóg. While she was combing her hair, the Earl of Desmond saw her and was overcome with love for her. He captured her cloak, which gave him control of her, and he made her his wife. Geróid Iarla, an enchanted son, was born from this union.[6] In the Expedition of Nera (*Echtra Nerai*) tale, or the Theft of the Cattle of Cuailnge (*Táin bó Cuailnge*) mythic cycle, a mortal named Nera was challenged to prove his courage by approaching a dead body on Samain.[7] Custom dictated that this was a dangerous thing to do because the *Sidhe*, a race of spirits sometimes called earth gods (*dei terreni*) and sometimes called the Tuatha Dé Danann, moved about freely on that night and were in control of the Dead who wander at that time. Being found near a dead person increased the risk of capture by the *Sidhe*. Nevertheless, Nera rose to the challenge and succeeded in tying a coil of twisted twigs around the leg of a body. His triumph was short-lived as he was caught up in adventures that drew him into following a fairy host into a fairy mound. He ended up in the palace of the Tuatha Dé Danann and was married to a fairy woman.[8]

A Special Case

The story of Cupid and Psyche is one of a god-human union. In spite of the objections of Venus, his mother, Cupid wedded Psyche, a mortal. She betrayed him, he left her, and she searched for him, knowing that she truly loved him. As a last resort, she approached Venus for help. Venus begrudgingly set impossible tasks for Psyche. The tasks, however, became a proving ground for Psyche's growth.

Psyche met each task with despair, but found help in accomplishing each. Ants helped her when Venus demanded that she sort out a batch of mixed grain. Reeds helped her when Venus told her to gather wool from a herd of ferocious sheep. An eagle, sent by Jupiter, helped her reach into the gorge of the River Styx to collect water in a jar. A tower, from which she prepared to throw herself, helped her to strategize the journey to the Underworld, where she secured some of Proserpine's beauty in a box.

Caitlín Matthews analyzes each of these tasks in her book *In Search of Woman's Passionate Soul*, and explains each as a metaphor for our own quest to find wholeness within ourselves. It is out of this wholeness that ordinary and non-ordinary relationships can form in healthy ways to feed our souls. In Matthews' interpretation, the ants teach us to sort out our ideas from those of others; the reeds teach us to use the resources of dreams and other states of consciousness to find aspects of our nature that need a voice; the eagle teaches us to be fearless; and the tower, which leads us to the box of beauty, teaches us to find and express our own beauty, not the idea of beauty imposed upon us by others.[9]

In the end, Cupid (Love) and Psyche (Soul) are wed before the gods and goddesses. Psyche is given a drink to make her immortal. The relationship between Cupid and Psyche ripened through Psyche's education via trial. It emerged in a higher form when they were married before the gods. The myth becomes a template for those who wish to explore the Spirit Mate as a way to promote personal development and enrich intimate relationships.

From the Workshop Journal: #2

The journaling exercises for the Spirit Mate workshop move into the realm of intimacy. Whether the relationship with the Spirit Mate is casual or evolves into one of merging or embodiment, issues of boundaries and trust arise, and it's beneficial to gain an understanding of present attitudes around intimacy before delving further.

Using the list from the first Journal exercise in Chapter 1, select those people with whom you are intimate.

— Journal

What do you consider intimacy to be? What is a healthy basis for intimacy? How do you characterize your intimate relationships? If you feel that you don't have any intimate relationships, why do you think that is so? Is there a pattern to your intimacy or non-intimacy? Is the issue of intimacy restricted to a significant other? Why or why not?

✤ Activity

Write a letter expressing gratitude to someone with whom you are intimate—a significant other or a dear friend. (Consider the kinds of things about them that you are grateful for. Do you possess these same qualities?)

Chapter 3

Saints & Lovers

"I love Christ into whose bed I have entered."
— Response of nuns at consecration[1]

While sex plays a major role in the Spirit Mate relationships of Baule men and women of the Ivory Coast, there is an interesting blend of the sexual and spiritual in the traditions associated with the Abrahamic religions. Christianity, Judaism and Islam all have sects wherein practitioners recognize the soul's longing to connect deeply and merge in ecstasy with the divine. The ecstasies of Christian mystics, Sufis and devout Jews have produced some of the most beautiful literature of love that inspires and guides the quest for divine connection.

It is important to consider what it is to be divine. For many, the connotation of 'divine' is strictly associated with 'God' or the 'Absolute'. But even the understanding of 'God' is different from tradition to tradition, and even within a tradition. The Merriam-Webster dictionary also includes 'godlike' and 'heavenly' in the definition of divine.[2] This is closely akin to the definition of 'supernatural', which relates to "an order of existence beyond the visible observable universe, esp.: of or relating to God or a god, demigod, spirit or infernal being."[3] For this investigation, the Spirit Mate belongs to the divine in the sense of 'godlike' (note the small 'g') and 'beyond the visible observable universe'. These denotations about a Spirit Mate might challenge traditional doctrine within the

Abrahamic faiths. However, when we stretch beyond the surface truth of these faiths to the deeper universals revealed through allegory, we have greater capacity for the magic life holds for us; we can expand and embrace more of the gift of life when we eliminate human, fear-based limitations.

The language of love in the memoirs, poems and religious books of the mystics and ecstatics of the Abrahamic tradition is often couched in the language of human sexual love. We read of the Bride, Bridegroom, Lover, Beloved and more. The following stories are atypical for most of the faithful. The passion and devotion to the sacred partner, or the divine partner, is of an intensity that tests the flesh and leads to extreme acts and changes in consciousness. These shifts in consciousness are responsible for contact with the supernatural, which results in renewed passion. Sometimes it is unclear if the passion drives these acts or if these acts drive the passion. Regardless, what follows are examples of people in orthodox Western religious traditions experiencing interaction with a spirit at a deep, personal, quasi-sexual level.

One of the most well-known of the Christian mystics is Saint Theresa of Avila (1515-1582). From an early age she sought the salvation that only a life dedicated to God could provide for her. A brief teenage interest in dresses and the company of the opposite sex ended when, against her father's wishes, she eased the agony of her love for God by entering the convent. In her writings, she confesses that her choice to enter the convent initially was more about seeking heaven over hell. However, she went on in her life to build an enduring relationship with her God, remaining in the convent for twenty-five years.[4]

During her time spent with 'Jesus as Bridegroom', Theresa discovered the comfort of orison (prayer). For her, the practice of orison was "an intimate, friendly intercourse with God, in which the soul expresses her love freely to Him who loves her."[5] The saint continued in her dedication to God in this way until 1555, when she encountered a statue of the Savior covered in wounds and read the *Confessions of St. Augustine*. These two experiences drove her more deeply away from the world toward a life that was focused only on God. In 1558, she experienced a rapture in which God spoke to her saying, "I do not want you any longer to converse with men but only angels."[6] This marked the period in her life when she experienced love-trances, visions and voices; at the same time she became more externally active in the world by founding numerous reform monasteries.[7]

St. Theresa's experience of her heavenly bridegroom brought her pleasure and pain. In describing one encounter she said that an angel of fire approached and "held in his hands a long golden dart, tipped with fire." The experience of the dart passing through her heart and into her bowels would "leave [her] aflame with divine love."[8] The Freudian implications cannot be ignored. She commented that "it was not a bodily, but a spiritual pain, although the body participated in it to a high degree."[9] Later, we will return to this double perception of body and spirit.

Another Christian mystic whose writings speak to us of divine love is Heinrich Suzo (1300-1366). At an early age he entered the Dominican Order and learned that the Church offered divine love in place of earthly love. While embracing this, he felt the need for a personal sense of love. One day this love came upon him and he felt it as the "original source of all good."[10] This love manifested as a feminine spirit who became "the Empress of my heart, the bestower of all gifts. In you I possess riches enough and all the power that I want. I care no longer for the treasures of the earth."[11] The name that Suzo gave his love was *Ewige Weisheit*, or Eternal Wisdom, and he preferred to relate to *Ewige Weisheit* in the form of the Virgin, young and beautiful.[12]

Having found this love, Suzo entered into a course of extreme asceticism in order to show his devotion, but also to rid himself of what he called 'evil tendencies' of the body. He experienced periods of discouragement punctuated by brief periods of ecstasy. Eventually he moved beyond ascetic methods and stepped out into the world to serve others as a completion of his sanctification.[13]

Saint Marguerite Marie (1647-1690) is best known for the revelation of the Devotion of the Sacred Heart of Jesus. From an early age, she found refuge from family circumstances in "austere penances, fasting, iron chains, sleeping on a board, and spending nights in prayer."[14] Her passion for the presence of God was "like a burning holy candle."[15] Her memoirs are filled with loving communications from Christ. "He said to her: 'I have chosen you as my bride; we promised each other faithfulness when you made me a vow of chastity. I pressed you to take that vow before the world had any part in your heart.'" Later she writes, "He showed me that He was the handsomest, the richest, the most powerful, the most perfect and accomplished of lovers..."[16] Saint Marguerite's daytime hours were focused so intensely on expunging weakness of the flesh that she often engaged in activities that challenged her to move beyond her frailty. Nights after succumbing to perceived imperatives (such as cleaning up a patient's vomit with her tongue), she was rewarded with contact with His sacred heart. Her passion for Jesus was incredibly intense, and she wrote of her bridegroom crushing her with the weight of his love. At her protest, she reports Him saying, "Let me do my pleasure. There is a time for everything. Now I want you to be the plaything of my love, and you must live without resistance, surrendered to my desires, allowing me to gratify myself at your expense."[17]

Like many Christian mystics, Juan De Yepes Y Alvarez entered an ordered community and practiced austerity and contemplation. His goal was to step away from the world and "tasteless material pleasures" in order to "attain union with the Beloved" as "lover (contemplative)."[18] Known to most as St. John of the Cross and for his 'dark nights of the soul', he worked to completely cut all ties to things binding him to this world. Out of years in solitude and

contemplation he communicates his experience of intimate union
with God in the following poem.

The Living Flame of Love[19]

Oh, living flame of love,
that tenderly stabs
my soul at its deepest center!
You are no longer elusive,
finish now, if you will,
rend the veil of this sweet encounter.

Oh, sweet cautery!
Oh, sweet wound that is gifted to me!
Oh, gentle hand! Oh, delicate touch
that is known in life eternal,
and repays all debts:
slaying, you have transformed death into life.

Oh, lamps of fire,
in whose brilliance
the deepest cave of the mind,
previously dark and blind,
with rare beauty,
heat, and light bestowed at the side of the Beloved.

How docile and affectionate,
you awaken in my breast
where in secrecy you alone dwell,
and in your delicious inhalation
overflowing with goodness and glory,
how delicately you love me!

Another example of ecstasy is found in the writings of Mechthild of Magdeburg. In her *Dialogue Between Love and the Soul*, she encourages "all virgins to follow the most charming of all, the eighteen year old Jesus, so He might embrace them." She continues, "Tell my Beloved that His chamber is prepared, and that I am sick with love for Him...Then he took the soul into His divine arms, and placing His fatherly hand on her bosom, He looked into her face and kissed her well."[20]

These few examples from Christian mysticism make it clear that some of the drive or passion that fuels the relationships these exceptional people had with the divine is borne on what we might call in modern technological terms, the 'carrier wave' of sexuality. Sexuality as an energy of sense and experience becomes not only the metaphor for discussing the relationship but also a component. Unlike the Baule, however, the relationship at the surface is not based on the self-serving gratification of physical desire and spousal control, but rather a desire to move beyond the needs of the flesh to the needs of the heart and soul. And there is a drive to ascend in ways beyond those of the ordinary Christian.[21] Through their relationships with a divine partner, mystics like Saint Theresa, Heinrich Suzo, Saint Marguerite, and others satisfied such tendencies as: the need for self-esteem, the need to cherish and devote oneself, the need for affection and support, the need for single-mindedness in passivity and action and the need for sensuous satisfaction.[22] Though their initial propensities were to remove themselves from the world, most mystics moved out into the world to take action. For example, St. Theresa founded monasteries and Suzo engaged in apostolic activities.[23] Ultimately, these were lives of service energized by an intimate relationship with the divine.

Also striking in these examples is the idiosyncratic language of personal experience; each partner in the mystical union speaks of the divine in a distinctive way, demonstrating the variations in conscious perception of the divine. Suzo speaks of his beloved as the Virgin or Eternal Wisdom. Saint Marguerite and Saint Theresa find that it is Jesus who is the Beloved, though Theresa also perceives an angel with a golden dart. Thus, even in traditions where agreement could be expected as to the nature of the divine personage, there is divergence based on gender and sexual preference.

Many of the Christian mystics engaged in behaviors that promoted changes in consciousness, such as pain, fasting, sleep deprivation and others. For certain ecstatics in other traditions, however, these extremes weren't the rule; yet the language of love for the Divine is hauntingly similar. One such example is the Indian mystic Kabir, who was born in the sacred Hindu city of Benares in 1440. Bound by neither Hinduism nor Islam, he lived the life of an ecstatic, seeking deeper and deeper rapture with the infinite.[24] Unlike his Christian counterparts, his life was not punctuated with asceticism or austerities, for which he found little use in his approach to the fathomless. He spoke to the common people and conveyed to them his reveries of a lover intoxicated with and ravished by God.[25] This love was expressed in poetry with lines like: "My Beloved One gleams like the lightning flash in the sky"[26] and, "O Sadhu! the simple union is best. Since the day when I met with my Lord, there has been no end to the sport of our love."[27]

In shamanic literature, the word *ecstasy* is used to describe the altered state of the shaman when he or she can fly.[28] This is quite different from our common use of the word connoting uncontrollable joy or some kind of intense emotional reaction. The root of the word is *ékstasis,* from the Greek, and signifies the separation of the shaman's spirit from his or her physical being during the shamanic journey. It is the shaman's ability to spiritually move which allows for the voyage to non-ordinary reality where contact is made with helping spirits.

In the foregoing examples of the mystics, orison and asceticism were the stimuli for ecstasy that allowed contact with the divine.

This sense of connection and intimacy can be summed up by the Sufi acknowledgment, *Ishk Allah Mabood Lillah*: God is Love, Lover, Beloved.

From the Workshop Journal: #3

The focus of journaling to this point has been on others, those we know, and how we relate to them. Hopefully, the concept of personal space and boundaries has surfaced and expanded to include a broader understanding of the patterns of approach-avoidance we employ as interpersonal strategies for relationships.

The Brazilian Spiritists dedicate much of their lives to spiritual study and communication with the spirits.[1] They have a longstanding tradition of dealing with all spirits in a compassionate loving manner. For them to work successfully to educate the living and the dead, the Spiritists advocate knowing oneself. This is good advice for all of us. As we know ourselves better, we can begin to use discernment in hearing answers from the spirit worlds. We learn to differentiate the voice of wishful thinking from the words of a loving helper.[2]

These exercises shift the focus to the self. In all spiritual work it is critical to know the workings of our internal landscape. This landscape is made up of our feelings, the stories we tell ourselves about ourselves, and our thoughts. A relationship with a Spirit Mate can affect one's inner workings; it has the potential to make you feel better about yourself.

In pursuing the following exercises, include the good, the bad and the ugly. The following questions were part of the opening of a sci-fi TV program called *Crusade,* and serve to reinforce that searching for a Spirit Mate relationship is a quest that begins with oneself.

⟶ Journal

Who are you?
What do you want?
Where are you going?
Whom do you serve?
Whom do you trust?

🌿 Activity

In summing up the answers above, write a Mission Statement for your life, what you believe to be your soul's journey and purpose in this life.

Chapter 4

Divine Election & the Imaginal Realm

"You must become a shaman and heal;
I love you, and you must be my husband."

— Spirit woman to Gol'dy man[1]

In shamanic literature, the Spirit Mate has often been called the celestial wife or celestial spouse. These terms locate this being in non-ordinary reality and also serve to define the relationship. Like Jesus or God of the Abrahamic religions, this spirit being often dwells in the heavenly realms, or the Upper World, and is thus divine. But where are these realms and how does one get there?

For the shaman, the world of non-ordinary reality is sectioned off into what Mircea Eliade has called cosmic zones. These zones—sky, earth and underworld—have been called the Upper, Middle and Lower Worlds and are particularly important for Siberian groups, who often represent these zones in artwork on their drums.[2] Traditions have located these non-ordinary worlds along an axis resembling a tree, in which the roots are in the Lower World, the trunk is in the Middle World and the crown is in the Upper World.[3] There are residents in each of these realms, and it is the shaman who establishes relationships with these beings in order to perform tasks and acquire information beneficial to the community. Many of the relationships forged by shamans with the helping spirits of the other worlds are critical, because the information provided through the relationships can have life and death consequences for the shaman's community.

It is challenging for Westerners to accommodate this idea of other worlds. Our rationalistic, materialistic culture has schooled us in habits of thought that immediately discount what we term *imaginary*.[4] The body of proofs from modern physics may be accepted on the level of intellect and propel us into reluctant acceptance of multiverses; however, the internalization of other worlds and the help dwelling therein is another question altogether.

In the early 1900s, the French philosopher and Iranologist Henri Corbin examined the visionary-initiatory writings of Sohravardi (12th century, Persia) who penned *The Crimson Angel*. While studying this tale, Corbin realized the inadequacy of language in locating the hidden land where certain initiatory experience takes place. The idea of 'where' is useless to the protagonist once he has crossed a boundary into the interior world. This is reminiscent of the experience of the shaman. During his journeys to the other worlds, he also crosses a barrier and enters into a space that is perceived as having a different order. Both the tale's protagonist and the shaman must learn to accept and function within a very different geographic terrain.

Corbin's studies culminated in the creation of the term *mundus imaginalis,* or the *imaginal,* to distinguish a very precise order of reality accessed by a precise mode of perception, and to distinguish it from the negatively connoted *imaginary*.[5] He found that the word *imaginary* had lost its power to convey information about reality and was a dismissive conclusion about what is not. As Corbin traversed the mystical literature he came to articulate three categories of universe: 1) the physical, sensory world; 2) the universe of pure archangelic intelligence; 3) the suprasensory world. These in turn correspond to the senses, the intellect, and the imagination, which in turn correspond to body, spirit, and soul. Each of these has an order of perception germane to it. For the corporeal, there is the visionary experience which encompasses something physically or objectively perceived. For the intellectual, there is the apprehension of an object in the mind without an image or form. And for the imaginative, something is experienced only inwardly in a psychic or spiritual sense.[6] Corbin's work ultimately provides a foundation for distinguishing the *imaginal* from the *imaginary*, allowing us access to a sacred version of the term.

This brief introduction to the imaginal is important because it informs the modern shamanic practitioner of the value of all the forms of perception available: the sensory, the intellectual and the imaginal. Each of these contributes to the work of the shamanic practitioner. It also stands as a defense for the validity of the shamanic journey, in that many times it is the active imagination that paves the way for subsequent spontaneous experiences in the cosmic realms.

Access to the cosmic realms is often gained using monotonous percussion. In many cultures, it is the beating of the drum that allows for the change in consciousness that is necessary for the shift to a new order of precise perception.[7] And, like the initiate in *The Crimson Angel,* a barrier has to be breached. For a journey to the Lower World, the barrier comes in the form of a tunnel that a shaman uses to descend into the earth. A journey to the Upper World is an upward flight that meets and pierces a barrier that can take many forms including ice, dirt, water or some other kind of membrane. Once this barrier has been breached, the shaman engages a different order of reality.

Although there are cases in which an individual actively seeks out initiatory relationships with the spirits of the cosmic realms, often the spirits breach the barrier between ordinary and non-ordinary reality to contact an individual with the news that he or she has been chosen to be a conduit for spiritual information and knowledge. This selection process, known as divine or religious election, provides more background for the Spirit Mate phenomenon in a shamanic context. Unlike the case of the Christian mystics who longed for connection to the Divine Being and acted in ways to accomplish the connection (asceticism, orison, etc.), the shaman-to-be is often the unwilling recipient of spirit attention and is reluctant to acknowledge and act upon the invitation.

This idea of being the 'chosen one' or the 'chosen people' of a divinity is not unfamiliar. In Greek mythology, for instance, there were those who were favored by the gods. Athena turned aside an arrow meant for Odysseus. Paris is saved from Achilles through the intervention of Aphrodite. In familiar Western faiths, the Jews are guided through the desert by Yahweh; Muhammad is chosen to receive the Qur'an from Allah; and Mary is favored by God to be the mother of Jesus. In the case of the would-be shaman, the pattern is contact by the spirit or spirits, followed by a period of confusion and sometimes dismay. This is one form of the classic shamanic illness, and the only way out is for the shaman to accept the help of the spirits in order to be healed.

Siberia

The word *shaman* comes from Siberia and has been translated as 'he or she who *knows*'. Because of this connection, it is appropriate to cite examples of Spirit Mates in the shamanic context from this region first. Siberia is a broad expanse of land with many cultures influenced by indigenous spiritualities as well as by the religions of Islam, Buddhism, and Hinduism. Ethnographic studies that trace Russian, and later Soviet, influence on the local populations show that a group's name for itself was often supplanted with the state's name for it. The word shaman is said to come from the Tungus people. This was a Soviet designation; the people called themselves the Evenki.

Siberia spans eight different time zones and is circled by dynamic mountain ranges: the Verkhoyansk, to the north and east; the Sayan, to the south; the Altai, also to the south; the Ural, to the west. Great rivers run through the land—the Ob, the Yenisey and the Lena. For much of the year, this land is frozen in the north on the Arctic Ocean. It warms gradually as it extends down through the taiga and into the steppes.[8]

The Siberian Tuvans, also known as the Uriankhai, tell the following story of the first shaman. There once was a man who fell in love with a celestial maiden. This man, Bö-Khân, was married to an ordinary reality woman at the time. When the celestial woman discovered his betrayal, she caused the earth to swallow up Bö-Khân and his wife. Later the maiden gave birth to the son of Bö-Khân, whom she abandoned to the care of a birch tree. The sap from the tree nurtured the boy who ultimately gave rise to a race of shamans called Bö-Khâ-näkn.[9] In this Spirit Mate story, there is the delightful inclusion of a spirit-child.

THE AYAMI

The Gol'dy, also known as the Nanai, live in the extreme east of Russia in the lower course of the Amur River. A Gol'dy shaman can only practice his vocation by and through his/her relationship with an *ayami*.[10] The *ayami* is a spirit who approaches a shamanic candidate and gives the power to shamanize. Lev Shternberg, a Soviet ethnographer researching in the late 1800s, learned through his interviews with a Gol'dy shaman that the man had resisted shamanhood and found little joy in it. The man had only become a shaman because he was approached by a beautiful and assertive spirit woman as he lay on his sickbed. With her dark, wavy tresses hanging to her shoulders, she told him, "I am your *ayami*, who has chosen you; I have taught your ancestors to be shamans; now I have come to teach you. You must become a shaman and heal; I love you, and you will be my husband; I will give you spirit-helpers; with their aid you will heal and help, and the people will feed us." The man was frightened but accepted after the *ayami* went on to add, "If you do not obey me, so much the worse for you; I will slay you."[11]

This invitation to become a shaman came upon the Gol'dy man after a period of shaman sickness in which he experienced aching in his body and head. After he acquiesced to the demands of the *ayami,* he recovered and they lived together as husband and wife. She acted as a tutelary spirit and came to him in the form of an old woman, a wolf or a winged tiger. The shaman described her entering him like smoke or steam. When that happened, all his actions became those of the *ayami.* According to the shaman, the *ayami* is a female for male shamans and male for female shamans because the *ayami* is equally man and woman.[12]

The Abasy

Shternberg found a similar situation among the Buryat people, who live around Lake Baikal. In this case, an ancestor spirit was responsible for taking the potential shaman's soul to heaven for instruction and orientation. But beyond this familiarization with heaven, the ancestor spirit introduced the candidate's soul to the "various ladies and daughters of the gods" in order to select a celestial spouse. "When the most solemn moment of the final engagement, constituting nothing more or less than the wedding of the shaman and his heavenly wife, had arrived—only then did he become a true shaman." Up until this time, the instruction of the shaman had proceeded through various levels under the guidance of older shamans.[13]

Shternberg also studied the Yakuts, a northeastern Siberian people. For the Yakuts, even ordinary people were tapped by male and female spirits for sexual encounters. M. Sleptsova, Shternberg's informant, talked extensively of the female *abasy* spirits who interfered with the ordinary reality relationships of young men with sweethearts and husbands with wives. Young male *abasy*-spirits likewise seduced young girls and wives. In the case of the shaman, however, there appears to be a divergence within the spirit world. A "master and mistress of the higher and nether worlds" appear to the shaman in dreams, but it is the sons or daughters of these higher beings who come to the shaman and engage in sexual intercourse with them. The timing of the appearance of this lover is critical. It must come before the shaman is called to treat a patient, if he is to heal successfully.[14]

Mexico[15]

The Valley of Mexico is the setting for the pueblo of San Francisco Tecospa, the site of a divine election resulting in a Spirit Mate union. In the mid-1900s, Don Soltero was contacted by the *enanitos*, who are the dwarf-sized rain deities. Rather than dreaming in his own bed like his Siberian counterparts, he was kidnapped by the *enanitos* and taken to their cave. There he was told that he would become a *curandero*, a healer receiving power directly from supernatural beings. When he refused, they beat him, whereupon he changed his mind and acquiesced. He was returned home with three curing tools: a staff, three curing stones and a spirit wife. According to Don Soltero, his spirit wife gives him the power to cure and to divine. She is a jealous being, and Don Soltero has had to concentrate his sexual energy on her alone to the neglect of his human wife.

Part of his relationship with the *enanitos* are Don Soltero's twice yearly mandatory meetings with entities called Yearly Deaths. In March, when the rains are about to begin, and again in October or November, when the rains have ended, Don Soltero 'dies' and goes to the cave of the *enanitos*. While there, he and other *curanderos* who have likewise been summoned are instructed by Yecacoatl, the chief *enanito*, in cures and curing implements (eggs, stones, herbs, etc.).

In the cases involving the *ayami*, *abasy* and *enanitos*, it is clear that the practitioner began his service as a shaman unwillingly. He was contacted by the Spirit Mate, sometimes through dreams, but did not come into full practicing or initiated status until the spirit relationship was acknowledged in some way. Once the relationship was acknowledged, the practitioner had the sufficient power and spiritual help to work on behalf of others.

From the Workshop Journal: #4

The shaman operates in a world that incorporates so much more than the human kingdom. The emphasis in the journal work now expands out to include all beings.

Shamans rely on their relationships with allies. Cornerstones to shamanic work are the Power Animal and the Teacher. But also important are the Spirit Mate, Ancestors and Nature Spirits. The shaman stands in the circle of these relationships and is the mediator of all the power embodied within on behalf of the community.

Showing respect for all beings—the four-leggeds, the creepy crawlies, the winged ones, the slithering ones, the swimming ones, the Stone People, the Standing People, the Green and Growing People—leads to other relationships. Think about all the other beings of the natural world: crystals, clouds, the elements, stars, planets, molecules, atoms. Think as big and as small as you can.

Consider the song of the shaman, "All that exists lives."[1]

— Journal

What is your relationship with the natural world? When you think of everything being alive, does your relationship change? Break this question down into as much detail as you wish. Are there places in which you experience intimacy with the natural world?

☙ Activity

Collect trash on a roadside, in a parking lot, at a playground. Make a list of other ways you might show the natural world that you care.

Chapter 5

Gender & the Call

"Once I went to my Spirit Mate depressed over reading of the brutal rapes and murders of two teenage girls in Canada. I was beginning to question the foundation of my own sexual drive, and I mentioned this to her. She said that sex is a way of intimately hurting someone or intimately loving someone. It is a vehicle of expression. How it is used is up to us. This simple thought calmed the misgivings I was having about my own sex drive."

— from author's journal, July 1995 (DR)

A thread winding through the Spirit Mate phenomenon is a sense of wholeness or completion. For humankind, this sense of wholeness involves the interplay and integration of polarities, one of the most sensitive being the masculine-feminine dyad. This pair is complicated by Euro-American notions of sex (anatomy), sexual behavior (who relates to whom; the penetration paradigm) and gender (societal roles and behaviors). Deeper than these notions are the metaphysical roots in which the dyad of masculine and feminine may contradict anatomy. In dealing with issues of the spirit and roles related to spirit work, masculinity and femininity are more accurately considered as creative principles.

To understand gender in this way, a reference to the *Kybalion* is useful. This text contains the teachings attributed to Hermes Trismegistus, the 'scribe of the gods', who allegedly lived in Egypt as a contemporary of Abraham. Many spiritual maxims have their origin in this book, which outlines the Seven Hermetic Principles.[1]

Though the language over the years has changed, these same principles can be found in most modern spiritual literature.

Of concern here is The Principle of Gender. Briefly, the *Kybalion* instructs that everything manifests with both masculine and feminine elements. "Gender is in everything; everything has its Masculine and Feminine Principles; Gender manifests on all planes."[2] Gender, derived from the Latin, means to "beget; to procreate; to generate; to create; to produce," and thus the sole office of gender is that of "creating, producing, generating, etc., and its manifestations are visible on every plane of phenomenon."[3] In relation to the shaman, "male and female forces can be used, balanced, adapted, and transformed by those who are skilled enough to handle their power."[4] This underscores a way of being for the shaman, who operates in The Way of the Healer—a power broker handling forces in such a way as to bring healing[5] to the world, a generator of change and a provider of hidden information.

With this spiritual grounding, the natural progression is to a better understanding of *gender*. This is clarified by the overarching term *gender culture* which refers to the way in which a given society constructs gender. By definition, *gender culture* is:

> *a society's understanding of what is possible, proper, and perverse in gender-linked behavior, and more specifically, that set of values, mores, and assumptions which establishes which behaviors are to be seen as gender-linked, with which gender or genders they are seen as linked, what is the society's understanding of gender in the first place, and, consequently, how many genders there are.*[6]

Gender and gender-defined behavior are part of an effort by society to exert social control, and different societies construct meaning for gender in different ways.

Gender for many groups is not the rigid two-gender construct pervasive in Euro-American thinking. Many indigenous groups—including those in North and South America, India, Polynesia, Siberia, Africa and Asia—operate on gender constructs that express multiple genders. Within various cultures, and during the lifetime of an individual, many gender roles and identities may be assumed within the community.[7] This *gender variance* has often coincided with the shaman's establishment of a Spirit Mate relationship.

Historical works have used the word *berdache* to describe a person living with multiple gender roles. The term is derogatory, as it was derived from the Arab *bardaj,* signifying a male prostitute or catamite, and derides an anatomical female living with masculine roles. More common in the literature now is the term *two-spirit people* which is used by those living alternative gender roles. In expanding gender classifications, the literature now uses the following: 'woman', a human with female anatomy who lives within the confines of woman's roles; 'man', a human with male anatomy who lives within the confines of man's roles; 'woman-man', a human with male anatomy who partially or completely adopts what is culturally defined as a woman's role; and, 'man-woman', a human with female anatomy who takes up the occupations of men.[8] All of these signify different genders. Yet, in another classificatory system, five forms of gender variance are recognized cross-culturally: hermaphroditic genders, two-spirit traditions, manly-hearted women, woman-marriage, boy-marriage, and rituals in which cross-dressing and/or other cross-gendered behaviors are institutionalized.[9]

In the lives of many people, gender variance is the natural state of affairs. In the binary system extant in Euro-American constructs, these shifts from 'one to the other' are called *gender reversals.* However, to be more accurate, in gender systems in which a shift is from "one to *another,*" the more appropriate term is *gender transformation.*[10] This transformation becomes relevant as we examine the next series of shamanic practitioners, who in various ways, take on the social behavior, dress and sometimes even language of another gender as they integrate power and a Spirit Mate relationship.

Broadly speaking, gender reversal or transformation serves several functions in religious mythology and ritual. In an earlier chapter, the idea of transformation was evident in the gods' abilities to change their appearances. Zeus became a swan and a bull; Thetis underwent multiple changes before resuming human form; Heimdall became a human man called Rig. The form may have shifted, but the essence did not.[11] Other meanings and results were also assigned to transformations. In some cases, as in the Dionysian rites of ancient Greece, the trading of dress between men and women in celebration of the god was an emulation of the cross-dressed deity which "perhaps [lifted] the participant out of his or her normal persona, by creating a special altered state for the religious rite."[12] In some Tantric sects of Hinduism and in Mahayana Buddhism, transformations may also be "associated with purification and elevation to a higher state." Ultimately, "it is not surprising that religious systems have often seen transformation of gender as linked with the process of coming closer to the Godhead, however it is construed."[13]

The Chukchi

The Chukchi are another of the shamanistic Siberian groups who demonstrate divine election through a strong relationship with a Spirit Mate. Among the Chukchi, as well as the Koryak, the initiand takes on the personality of the Spirit Mate so strongly that he or she literally changes gender.[14] The anatomical male shaman becomes female in gender and exhibits this role by a change in dress and hair style to that of a woman; (s)he does women's work and speaks in a special women's language. For all intents and purposes, the male shaman becomes female. This extends to other aspects of social roles, including the ordinary reality marriage in which (s)he now marries a man.[15] Women, too, have been known to undergo the same kind of gender transformation. The one case that is on record reports a middle-aged widow who upon election cut her hair like a male, dressed like a male and behaved like a male in language and hunting. She married a girl and handled the delicacies of ordinary reality sexual activity using a reindeer calf muscle. These couples had children legitimized through adoption or 'produced' in other extramarital, creative ways.[16] Although stigmatized for being unusual, both male and female transformed shamans gained extraordinary spirit power.[17]

The Mapuche[18]

The Mapuche are the indigenous population of Chile. Confined to several reservation regions, many maintain their traditional spiritual practice and become *machi.* Over the years the role of the *machi* has taken on political nuances, but the *machi* still act as intermediaries for humans in order to bring health and balance.

Each *machi,* regardless of anatomical sex, connects with the power of the forest spirits through *foki,* or vines, and with that of the sky spirits, the *filew.* The *filew* is the *machi's* personal, possessing spirit husband, and it is up to each practitioner to seduce this spirit and become bridely during the initiation process in order to gain knowledge. Thus, during the initiation ceremony, all *machi,* regardless of sex, are brides. Anthropologist Ana Mariella Bacigalupo reports that "As spiritual brides, *machi* participate in the cosmic process of fertility and reproduction, which holds priority over conflicts with their personal sexual and reproductive lives."[19]

Machi also embody the masculine element. Once they have seduced their spirit husbands, they climb the *rewe,* a step-notched pole that serves as the axis mundi or altar for their spirits. This is equated to mounting a horse to ride to the sky. Riding, horsemanship, and lifting are associated with warfare, a very masculine activity. According to Bacigalupo, the "*machi* view themselves as masculine mounted warriors who defeat evil, illness, and suffering."[20] The *machi* work to embody the four different aspects of their deity Ngunechen: Old Man, Old Woman, Young Man and Young Woman. Through this embodiment, they express dyadic relationships of wisdom-fertility, age-youth, war-healing, authority-nurture, and parenthood-childhood. In their healing activities, the *machi* exhibit varied gendered relationships with their spirit husbands, relationships that are embodied and ensouled.

Once again we are reminded of the shaman's relationship to power. Spirit power is conducted into ordinary reality through the shaman who embodies more balanced and more complete masculine and feminine principles. These principles, for some shamans, play out in ordinary reality as gender transformations, though that is not a requirement of or for a Spirit Mate relationship. What results from this relationship is the possibility of expanded expression that communicates outside the typical boundaries of gender culture.

From the Workshop Journal: #5

The shaman is the 'hollow bone' standing between ordinary reality and non-ordinary reality. It is the shaman who goes to the spirits and seeks knowledge to bring back help to his community. The importance of nurturing relationships with helping spirits cannot be over emphasized. These are the relationships the shaman relies upon to do his work of healing or acquiring knowledge. To engage in shamanism is to use the spirits. If one is not using the spirits, one is not doing shamanism.

⚊ Journal

Are you aware of helping spirits in your life? In what ways does that help appear? How have they helped you?

✸ Activity

Develop and perform a two-minute ceremony or ritual acknowledging your spiritual help.

⚊ Journal

The journal question below assumes that the respondent has engaged in shamanic journeying and is aware of his or her specific helping spirits. Those who attend the Spirit Mate workshop must have journeying experience and be aware of their helping spirits, usually in the forms of a Power Animal and a Teacher.

What is your relationship to the spirit world? What is your relationship to your helping spirits? What's good about it? How might you work to improve it?

✱ Journey

You may wish to journey to your helping spirits and ask for a ceremony to acknowledge them, to celebrate their presence in your life. Ask if there is anything that they would like you to include such as candles, fragrance/incense, or food offerings.

🌿 Activity

Perform the ceremony you received from your helping spirits.

— Journal

Write a poem or a song for each helping spirit.

Chapter 6

Inspirational Possession

"As the days of early summer passed, I found myself awakening earlier and earlier, a perfect time to switch on the drumbeat tape and journey to my Spirit Mate. Our friendship deepened, and it seemed almost essential that we do something to formalize our relationship. We exchanged rings and the bond seemed to be cemented. My interaction with her began to work a kind of magic on me. I was immersed in a love which permeated my physical, emotional and spiritual being. The pain I had been feeling over the rejection by my last girlfriend was sinking out of my awareness. In its place a strong but quiet joy surfaced that was solid and dependable, something to hold on to."

— from the author's journal, July 1995 (DR)

Humans swim in a sea of power; individuals constantly negotiate power within their relationships. People relate to each other by exerting power, sharing power or giving up power. The ways in which these exchanges take place relate to the boundaries each person has and how well the person knows and respects himself and others. When people are unclear about who they are, what they stand for and how they wish to conduct themselves in the world, personal boundaries become permeable— misplaced power seeps in or personal power becomes lost. Being the master of oneself and one's behavior in the world is the best strategy for plugging up the holes in one's boundaries and living a life governed by one's own will.

Being in relationship with the spirits demands a degree of self-knowledge that the human practitioner must cultivate in order to recognize what is and what is not of the self. And, when the 'not self' is encountered, it is essential to exercise discernment in order to characterize the type of influence that is being exerted. While it is important for the shaman to be the 'hollow bone', it is also critical that the shaman knows what is passing through him or her in the role as a power conduit for the community.

Possession

In many ways, language characterizes beings and the ways that beings can influence a living human or place. The words *attaching, possessing, obsessing, overshadowing* and *influencing* are somewhat synonymous. They all highlight the fact that a living human or host is being affected by an errant or wandering spirit (of a deceased human), an Earthbound entity, a ghost, a discarnate (without a physical body), a noncarnate (a being who never had a physical body) or the soul parts of another (who may or may not be dead). The environment may reflect this spiritual activity via a *psychic imprint*, when the energy of an event is impressed upon the place and replays there, or a *haunting*, when a spirit appears and actively associates with a place. These entities typically have their own agendas and try to use their proximity to a living human to achieve their own goals which may or may not be beneficent. Possession or attachment of this nature is called *involuntary* possession; the human host is usually unwittingly involved.

For some, "possession…is a *belief*, a cultural belief, a shared and not idiosyncratic belief. Insofar as the behavior involves acting out a personality which is believed in, concerning which there are shared expectations, to that extent surely 'possession states' cannot exist in societies where such beliefs are absent."[1] Thus, some consider that possession can only occur in a society where there is a belief in the possibility. There are a number of societies in which a specific kind of possession plays a role in relationship to the Spirit Mate. In these societies, a practitioner connects with a Spirit Mate and voluntarily allows the spirit to enter into the body in order to perform useful tasks for the community. The spirit husbands or wives, like the Animal Spirit helpers or Teachers of the shaman, offer help to the shaman usually in the form of power for healing and divination. The shaman is sometimes reluctant to accept this power, knowing the responsibility that accompanies it. For the shaman who answers the call, it is not always an easy choice and sometimes comes on the heels of a serious illness.

Many shamans in traditional societies join with their helping spirits—oftentimes the Spirit Mate—to conduct rituals and perform healings. This union of a shaman with a helping spirit occurs during an altered state of consciousness or trance, and has been called *merging* by some. At its most intense level, it is *voluntary* or *inspirational* possession. One of the best known examples of inspirational possession used for healing is Rubens Faria. Faria lives in Brazil and channels the spirit of Doctor Fritz, a medical doctor who was born in Munich, studied in Poland and died in Estonia in 1915. Since 1947, Fritz's spirit has been working through various individuals, the latest being Faria. Faria treats hundreds of people a day as Dr. Fritz, using injections of turpentine and operating without anesthesia.[2] The celebrated John of God is another example of inspirational possession.

In the Spirit Mate phenomenon, some practitioners allow themselves to experience a kind of *inspirational* possession by a spirit spouse in order to act in spiritual ways on behalf of their communities. Unlike the form of possession that I. M. Lewis outlines, in which those relegated to a subservient or marginal level of a society become "possessed" and are elevated to a new status via a highly structured pattern, these practitioners are not seen to be manipulating a social hierarchy through their possession behavior.[3] In fact, for the practitioners of Burma, possession behavior originally marked a loss of social status. It is only in more recent times that formal recognition of the calling has been a source of pride for some, and practitioners from modern Myanmar gather to have their practices evaluated by elders according to a code of ethics.[4]

The Saora

In the latter half of the 1940s, Verrier Elwin studied a group of people in the eastern Indian hills known as either the Saora or Savara, and observed that a number of their religious functionaries operated with the assistance of a spirit spouse. These relationships were not primarily sexually driven, but rather were meant to inspire and instruct. The spouses acted as tutelaries, meeting the human partner in dreams and accompanying him or her in the performance of sacred duties.[5] At specific ceremonial times, the garb of the spirit spouse cum tutelary was donned by the functionary who entered into trance and merged with the spirit. In trance, the functionary was able to communicate with the spirit world.[6]

For the Saora, the acquisition of the Spirit Mate typically occurs during adolescence. The adolescent is suddenly shifted into the spiritual world of the adult and becomes unbalanced, often wandering in a witless state of dissociation. This state may bring on a surge of resistance to the change from youth to adult, but once the resistance fades the wits return, and the dissociative state, the trance, is used in a controlled way for ceremonial purposes.[7] During the trance state, the human becomes possessed, normally by his or her own tutelary first, then other gods and ghosts.[8]

One elderly Saoran man named Kintara recounted his initial introduction to his Spirit Mate. At the age of twelve, "a tutelary girl called Jangmai came to me in a dream and said, 'I am pleased with you; I love you. I love you so much that you must marry me.'"[9] Kintara refused until Jangmai sent her dog [a tiger] to bite him, whereupon he capitulated. Another tutelary approached him on the heels of this agreement, but Jangmai jealously put a stop to it and sent Kintara wandering without his memory for a year. Finally, his parents called in a shaman who spoke in trance as Kintara's tutelary. The tutelary said, "Don't be afraid. I am going to marry him. There is nothing in all this; don't worry, I will help the boy in all his troubles."[10]

As part of his marriage to his tutelary, Kintara received a rice pot and clothing for his new spirit spouse. The rice pot was dedicated to her and hung in the rafters of his home. As with all functionaries who work with a spirit spouse, a physical object, in this case a pot, serves as the focus for the tutelary's presence.[11] The clothing of the tutelary is likewise kept as a bundle in the roof. Kintara reports that "Jangmai's possessions are always there, hanging from the roof, and when she asks for them I take them down and show them to her. Often at the Harvest Festivals she comes for her colored cloth; I put it on and dance in her name."[12]

Both men and women can be approached to be spiritual functionaries through marriage to a tutelary spirit. This marriage to a tutelary does not exclude the possibility of marriage to a human spouse, although there may be some negotiation that ensues as the relationships are established. There may even be some societal controls exerted as in Kintara's case where duties and behaviors were delineated. He reports that in his wedding bed Jangmai came upon him and spoke to his new human wife Dasuni in this way: "'Now you are going to live with my husband. You will fetch his water, husk his rice, cook his food; you will do everything, I can do nothing. I must live below. All I can do is to help when trouble comes. Tell me, will you honour me or no, or are you going to quarrel with me?' Dasuni answered, 'Why should I quarrel with you? You are a god-wife and I will give you everything you need.' Jangmai was pleased at that and said, 'That is well. You and I will live together as sisters.' Then she said to me, 'Keep this woman as you have kept me. Do not beat her. Do not abuse her.' So saying, she went away."[13]

Spirit husbands also communicate to human husbands. One man named Somra quarreled with his shamanin wife. (In the literature on the Saora the term *shamanin* is used to indicate a female functionary while *shaman* indicates a male functionary.) The report is clear that Somra only quarreled once. After abusing his wife, Somra became ill and thought he was going to die. He had to ask his wife what was happening. "Her husband, her tutelary, came to her from the Under World and said to me, 'If you ever abuse your wife like that again, I shall take her away. I am pleased with her; that's why I married her, and I'd very much prefer to have her with me here. She may be yours but she is also mine...from today, never abuse or beat her, or I will come at once and take her away.'"[14] Problems of this nature that require the intercession of the spirit husband are the exception, and most husbands live "happily with their shamanin wives and are often genuinely proud of the position that they win for themselves in tribal life."[15]

The classification system that categorizes spiritual functionaries for the Saora is complex and highly specialized. Within the overarching Kuranmaran category alone there are five subgroups.[16] Some of these practitioners are married to a tutelary and others are not. Some learn in dream and trance, while others learn from other shamans. Some can perform great rituals and others have more restricted duties. There are somewhat fewer classifications for shamanins, but the same kinds of limitations apply as for their male counterparts. Occasionally, a shaman or shamanin may marry two or three tutelaries.

While possession in the Saoran case seems somewhat heavy-handed initially ("You will marry me!"), there is evidence that it is of an *inspirational* or *voluntary* nature. Once the shaman or shamanin has accepted the call to the work, he or she appears to easily go into trance and act as the conduit for the spirits. Elwin reported embarrassment when a shamanin would slip into trance upon hearing his gramophone.[17]

The stories of shaman/shamanins indicate that tutelary spirits come from the Under or Lower World. For the Saora, the Underworld is the place of the Afterlife for the ancestral dead and the home of several other classes of spirits of which the tutelaries rank at the top as more powerful and more respectable.[18] These beings give help; recall Jangmai's conversation to Kintara's parents and his ordinary reality wife Dasuni. The tutelaries provide teaching for the practitioner, allowing him to perform sacred duties that include rites for the dead, officiation at high ceremonies, diagnosis and cure of disease, divination, organization and hospitality. Shaman/shamanins report that contact with their tutelaries is a beautiful thing.[19]

Contact with other spirits, such as those of ancestors, is often dark and can leave the shaman/shamanins fatigued; the dead are more exhausting than others.[20] Yet, the human vessel for the Spirit Mate is very conscious of his or her relationship to the spirits. In spite of certain hardships, in the case of one functionary, she "works ceaselessly, for she is inspired not only by pride in her profession, but also by her love for the tribal community she serves."[21]

The Burmese

The cult of the *Thirty-Seven Nats* coexists with Buddhism in Myanmar, formerly known as Burma. The focus of the cult is on the propitiation of *nats*, spirits of deceased human beings who by virtue of having died a violent death, become *nats*. According to this system, these spirits can be responsible for good or bad, and it is the job of a human functionary, the *nat kadaw*, to help keep the *nats* pleased so that the bad may be avoided. In return for appropriate tending, the *nat* provides the functionary with protection, the power to divine, and help in healing. This is unlike the Buddhist approach that engages in direct confrontation with the *nats*. The functionary operating within the *nat* cultus is used as a vehicle to give voice to a troublesome *nat* with the assistance of a *nat* spirit spouse—an ecstatic practice of embodiment and trance. A Buddhist functionary, commonly called an exorcist, speaks with a *nat*—a verbal technique.[22]

Traditionally, a woman was approached by a *nat* who informed her that he had fallen in love with her and wished to marry her. The woman resisted because marrying a *nat* was a shameful thing for three main reasons. First, marrying a *nat* implied a sexual relationship with him. Secondly, the *nat* marriage painted a woman as sexually immoral and promiscuous. Thirdly, when the *nat* possessed his wife, she danced in public and that was also frowned upon.[23] Of a more practical concern was the cost of a marriage to a *nat*. It took a great deal of time to collect the funds to properly conduct a marriage ceremony. More recently, however, magical events around a woman may open her to the opportunities of spirit, and she willingly undertakes the study to become a *nat kadaw* from an already established *nat kadaw*. The *nat* whom she will marry is chosen through a kind of lottery.[24] One *nat kadaw* recently interviewed was quite proud of her profession and displayed her license to practice as a "Spiritual Technician," which was granted by the Myanmar Ministry of Culture's Performing Arts Department.[25]

Often the *nat kadaw's* first exposure to a *nat* is during a *nat* festival called a *nat pwe*. In the excitement of the festivities, he or she becomes possessed and dances with abandon. As with the Saora, this occurs early in life. Having been overcome with the presence of the *nat*, a *nat kadaw* is called in to divine which *nat* has been attracted to the girl's or boy's beautiful butterfly-soul and wishes to establish a marriage. Once the *nat* has been discovered, an engagement is established which may last many decades until the formal marriage ceremony can be performed. During the engagement, the electee is allowed to perform tasks and learn from an established *nat kadaw*. At the time of Melford Spiro's study in the early 1960s, most of the humans with spirit spouses were female, though 3-4 % were male and labeled as transvestites.[26] All of the human spirit spouses dress as women,[27] resembling the practice of the *machi* who, regardless of anatomy, dress as brides to attract the *filew*, or sky spirits.

The wedding to a *nat* takes place at a *nat* palace and requires the preparation of bridal chambers, fees and an orchestra. Since *nats* may be married to multiple human wives, a *nat kadaw* married to the *nat* of the betrothed dances the *nat's* special dance to initiate the ceremony. The bride dons bridal garments—those clothes associated with the *nat*—and enters into the bridal chamber where there are beds for the bride and groom. It is possible that the bride may marry brother *nats* and in that case, a bed for each groom is prepared. At the core of the ceremony, the bride's butterfly-spirit is put to sleep so that her/his *nat* groom's butterfly-spirit may join with it. In this way the wedding is consummated and the bride ultimately goes into seclusion with her/his *nat* husband for seven days.[28]

The Temiar

The Temiar are a people who live in the Malaysian rainforest, inhabiting land along the five major rivers that flow from the mountainous backbone of the peninsula. They are a people known for their dreams and the power that flows from their dreams through song. They are grouped with the Semai and are often classified as the Senoi. In recent years various dream theories have been ascribed to them which have been discredited by researchers.[29] However, although the Temiar don't actively practice what has been called Senoi Dream Theory, they have an important dream practice that inspires their healing and ritual singing sessions.

The inspirited quality of the Temiar landscape permeates Temiar cosmology. All components of their universe have bounded and unbounded spirit and all have upper- and lower-portion souls. Due to this homology, human and nonhuman entities can interact, particularly during sleeping dreams, when the detachable upper-portion soul of the human, the head soul, wanders and meets other souls. During these meetings, a nonhuman soul that the head soul encounters can express a desire to become the dreamer's spiritguide, solidifying the relationship by giving the dreamer a song.[30]

Once a dreamer has been given a song, he is said to have *halaa'*, or adeptness.[31] Having *halaa'* enables one to diagnose and treat illness,[32] and the song is used as the means through which the dreamer reestablishes his connection to his spiritguide. He then can act as a medium, and through trance he is able to translate the knowledge and power from the spiritguide to the community via *kahyɛk,* a kind of clear spirit liquid he generates during healing ceremonies.[33]

The relationship of the medium and spiritguide is expressed in multiple roles somewhat akin to the multiple roles of the Mapuche *machi.* While there isn't a gender basis for the roles, there is a balanced hierarchy that expresses in numerous ways. The spiritguide is the child and the human/dreamer is the father. The human/dreamer is the student and the spiritguide is the teacher. This creates a power balance between the spiritguide and the human in that child-teacher becomes equivalent to father-student.[34] The Temiar term for the spiritguide, *gonig,* meaning consort, reveals another aspect of the relationship: the spiritguide of the medium is not only a child and teacher, but also a lover. In one dream story, the dreamer reports, "I sleep with her at night in my dreams, but in the morning my bed is empty."[35]

Longing is a theme in some of the songs that connect a medium to his spiritguide. Here is an echo of the longing of the Christian mystics. For the Temiar, longing reflects not only desire but also the transitory nature of the relationship. An entity will speak primarily in cross-gendered persona to the wandering head soul of a Temiar. He or she will speak saying, "I come to you, I desire you. I want to be your teacher, I want to call you father."[36] It is during performance of the dream relationship through the ritual use of the dream song that the medium connects through trance to his spiritguide.

"The potential emptiness of longing is filled by the presence of the emergent spiritguide."[37]

Women have been known to become mediums but mediumship is almost exclusively expressed by males. This contrasts to the Burmese *nat kadaw*. And while it is agreed that any male can become a medium, not all do. Males receive songs from their late teens and onward.[38]

Like the Burmese and the Saoran examples, the trance-dancing ceremonies of the Temiar enable the embodiment of the spiritguides. However, the Temiar do not marry their spiritguides. But like *machi* brideliness, their ritual performances serve to entice and attract the spiritguides, particularly the seductive sway, a use of "studied and intentional" movement.[39] There is a distinct presence of sexual tension expressed via longing that is at play. As one Temiar woman medium remarked, "There is a male spirit of the fruits that desires to sleep with me. Even when I dream, he's there. After a while one doesn't feel right, one's heart is shaky, one thinks only of him, one wants to go off into the jungle, one's spirit is drawn to the jungle. I must participate in a singing ceremony, only then can I stand it. We sing and dance, the male spirit of the fruit trees alights on the leaf ornaments, and I am transformed."[40]

Again as in the experience of the Saora and Burmese, the Temiar practitioner engages his or her spirit spouse through trance. During the throes of the trance, the spouse enters the body of the human mate and acts by speaking or dancing in ecstasy. The Saoran shamans/shamanins, the *nat kadaw* and the Temiar dreamer do not journey to the spirits, rather the spirits come upon them. In the view of Eliade and others, this excludes them technically from the classification of 'shaman', which necessitates that a functionary journey, that is, travel to the other cosmic zones. This by no means negates the importance of these functionaries to their communities, nor is it a comment on their efficacy.[41]

Unlike those Chukchi who permanently merge or unite with the spouse and experience a complete transgendered existence, both the Saoran (male) shamans and Burmese (male) *nat kadaw*s unite in voluntary or inspirational possession for a limited time, expressing a socially acceptable yet somewhat limited transgendered identity through the clothing of the spirit spouse.[42] This is distinguished yet further when considering the *machi* who behave in transgendered ways during ritual as well as in ordinary life, operating simultaneously with multiple genders, expressing in dress and action the broader incorporation of the four-part deity Ngunechen.

From the Workshop Journal: #6

What does it mean to have a spiritual experience? Some would say that 'spiritual' equates to 'mystical'. But what does mystical mean?

One opinion comes from James H. Leuba, who wrote *The Psychology of Religious Mysticism* in 1925. He takes the term to most usefully mean "any experience taken by the experiencer to be a contact (not through the senses, but 'immediate', 'intuitive') or union of the self with a larger-than-self, be it called the World-Spirit, God, the Absolute, or otherwise."[1]

Beyond this concept based commonly on the supernatural as a kind of 'good divinity', we can also recognize that there can be negative encounters with the supernatural. These encounters are often classified as 'evil' or even 'Satanic', especially from an Abrahamic traditional point of view. (A reminder here—the Brazilian Spiritists act compassionately. They call the beings engaging in negative behavior with humans 'suffering beings'.)

Here is some language to help you in considering your experiences.[2]

Divine Contact

- Confirming (general sense of presence/sacredness, specific awareness)
- Responsive (you are aware of the divine and it is aware of you)
- Ecstatic (intimate and affective contact with the divine)
- Revelational (divine gives you information and/or you become an agent of the divine)

Diabolic Contact

- Confirming (general sense of presence/evil, specific awareness)
- Responsive (you are aware of evil and it is aware of you)
- Terrorizing (intimate and loathsome contact with the diabolic)
- Possessional (diabolic gives you information and/or you become an agent of the diabolic)

Journal

What is the nature of your relationship to the supernatural as defined above? What experiences—high points or 'dark nights'— have you had that inform your relationship?

Journal

Write about the ways you have connected with God, World-Spirit, the Absolute and/or the supernatural from childhood to the present.[3]

Let's return to the cry of the Sufi. *Ishk Allah Mabood Lillah.* The Sufis are not the only ones to think of the Absolute in this way. Practitioners of Bhakti Yoga—a kind of Yoga based on mystical devotion—need only repeat the name of God to be led to the ecstasy where the Love, Loving and Beloved are one.[4]

Ishk Allah Mabood Lillah.
God is Love, Lover, Beloved.

— Journal

Write about the implications for your personal experience of ecstasy if you were to open to the perception suggested by this phrase.

Chapter 7

Mysticism, Ecstasy and the Anthropos

"During one visit, a shrouded being appeared before us. My Spirit Mate told me that death is the beginning of a new life; it is a birth. We pulled the shroud from the figure and were flooded by the brightest light, pure, brilliant, blinding. We were awash in it. Suddenly we were surrounded by angels and cherubs, seemingly hundreds. We sprouted wings ourselves. I saw that she was an angel, and that I was one as well."

— from author's journal, July 1995 (DR)

The foundation for any exploration of the Spirit Mate phenomenon resides in an understanding of the words applied to it. It has been called both *mystical* and *ecstatic* and thus further discussion may be useful. In addition to the definition offered by James Leuba in Chapter Six, mysticism, or the mystical, has also been described as "the preparation for, the consciousness of, and the effect engendered by...a direct and immediate transformative contact with the divine presence."[1] Mysticism has also been identified as "a doctrine or belief that a direct knowledge or immediate perception of the ultimate reality, or God, is possible in a way different from normal sense experience or ratiocination."[2] These definitions are applicable to the shamanic journey, which is a method for engaging a paranormal means of perception that allows for the direct experience of the world of spirits and the Ultimate in non-ordinary reality; this perception is promoted by relationships with helpers dwelling in those realms, including the Spirit Mate.

These beings are recognized as deities in different belief systems, and contact with them is transformative.

If contact is an intentional union of God and human in which the two maintain distinction one from the other, the experience is said to be *mystical uniting*. If on the other hand, the distinction between God and human becomes blurred and a deeper union is expressed, it is said to be *mystical identity*.[3] Flowing from this union, be it of the *uniting* or *identity* typology, is knowing (gnosis) and loving, each a part of unitive expression, though some mystics stress the superiority of love.[4] Generally speaking, the shaman or shamanic practitioner maintains a sense of distinction from the Spirit Mate, although in some cases, the practitioner forms a more permanent or deeper union in which the identity of the Spirit Mate is expressed in day-to-day matters.

The shaman journeys and merges with helping spirits. As Mircea Eliade noted, the shaman is familiar with the territory of the spirits and is able to visit and bring back knowledge from that realm and apply it, typically to circumstances extant in a community context.[5] He locates the wandering herd needed for food, compounds plant medicines or extracts harmful spirit intrusions from a sick person. In following the Path of the Healer, the shaman or shamanic practitioner works with power. Power on this path has been defined as energy plus intelligence, love and ethics.[6] When the shaman stands solidly in union with his helpers, his heart generates a dynamo of energy which provides a pattern to which the patient can entrain.[7] This is why it is often said that it is the attitude of the shaman that matters more than the attitude of the patient in healing. Thus, there is unitive expression of the shamanic practitioner's relationship with the spirits in the fields of power, knowledge and love, particularly when love is viewed not only as the universal love known as 'compassion' that drives healing work, but also as the love the shaman has for his or her helping spirits, among these being the Spirit Mate.

While mysticism embodies the possibility or belief in contact, ecstasy addresses the actual practice or experience. Ecstasy has been defined as both "the seizure of one's body by a spirit and the seizure of a human by a divinity."[8] Based on the nature of the communications emanating from the connection, additional distinctions can be made between *shamanic ecstasy, prophetic ecstasy* and *mystical ecstasy.* In the first, the communications of the shaman relate to the world of spirits; the shaman communicates with a number of spirits: the dead (the Ancestors and others), Animal Spirits, Teachers and the Nature Spirits. For the prophet, the communication is from the Absolute; the prophet speaks for God. And, in the case of the mystic, there is an identity with God and thus communications of *mystical ecstasy* are considered speaking as God.[9] While these distinctions seem hard and fast, the shaman in modern times, if he recognizes a Supreme Being, classifies It as a spirit, and certain beings, Teachers in particular, as deities, that is, gods or goddesses. Reports from students with strong Christian backgrounds indicate that their journey work sometimes brings them into contact with Jesus, who is a recognized aspect of the three-part deity (Father, Son, Holy Spirit). For some indigenous groups, there may be no concept of an Absolute, and messages from the other worlds don't even include the possibility of God, in the Western sense, as a source.

In the discussion of ecstasy, two distinct traditions flow forth and are identified by emotion and intuition.[10] These compare with the mystical expressions of loving and knowing respectively, as well as to the concepts of *mystical unity* and *mystical identity.* Emotion reflects the belief that the human and the Ultimate are distinct entities and their connection is something to be gained through the ecstatic experience of *communion.* Intuition reflects the belief that the human and the Ultimate share an ontological identity and that the awareness of such is regained and recognized as *union.* Once again, the lines are blurred and varying degrees of emotion and intuition inform the ecstatic experience of the shaman and shamanic practitioner.

Mystical Union and Kabbalah

Jewish mysticism emerged in one form known as Kabbalah in the 12th century in Provence. Books credited to Moses de León were circulated late in that period and became known as *Ha-Zohar ha-Qadosh,* or *The Holy Zohar,* and are the basis of Kabbalah. Presented in novel form, the writings are a commentary on the Torah and tell the tales of a wandering man named Rabbi Shim'on. Throughout the book, the personality of God is revealed through the ten *sefirot,* each of them a fundamental quality or emanation of the divine.[11] In pursuing the teachings of the *Zohar,* and following the path laid out by the *sefirot,* the student is encouraged to repair the original sin of lost intimacy with God and regain cosmic consciousness.[12]

One depiction of the *sefirot* is as a cosmic tree growing downward from its roots above. This is reminiscent of the shaman's tree that connects the Lower, Middle and Upper Worlds as discussed in Chapter Four.[13] Shamans, too, are known for the use of inverted trees with roots planted in the air. The inverted tree is one of the most archaic symbols of the World Tree.[14]

The *sefirot* are also represented as an androgynous divine body—two sides, two poles—male and female in the dynamic of the creative act. The kabbalist uses the ten *sefirot* as platforms for delving into the hidden nature of God in order to "become the 'site' of the Sacred Marriage of heaven and earth."[15] One of the ways Kabbalah speaks is through the language of the divine marriage. As one follows the tree from the roots in heaven down to the crown which is earthly manifestation or Presence, the Infinite or *Ein Sof* (aka *Keter* or *Ayin,* Nothingness) becomes differentiated into *Hokhmah* (Wisdom) and *Binah* (Understanding, the womb of the Divine Mother). At this point on the tree, conception takes place between *Binah* and *Hokhmah* and the seven lower *sefirot* come into being.[16] These lower seven are: *Hesed* (Love), *Gevurah* (Power, aka Din or Judgment), the central *sefirah Tif'eret* (King, Beauty, also the rabbinical name for God), *Netsah* (Eternity), *Hod* (Splendor), *Yesod* (Foundation, aka *Tsaddiq* or the Righteous One) and *Shekhinah* (Presence, Queen, aka *Malkhut* or Kingdom). Kabbalists see the goal of human spiritual life as the union of *Shekhinah,* the divine feminine and daughter of *Binah,* with *Tif'eret* through virtuous actions which stimulate *Yesod* to bring about the union of the divine couple.[17] Through Kabbalah, heaven and earth can unite as well as *Tif'eret* (the King) and *Shekhinah* (the Queen). And through this unification of the characteristics of the divine within each human, we can become vessels of divine power and creativity.[18] These marriages with the divine are replicated in the marriage between humans, which mirrors the essence of the divine marriage.[19] Though the *sefirot* appear to be multiple and independent, all of them are ultimately one.[20] This is mystical union.

When the kabbalist becomes the site of the Sacred Marriage, the path is laid out to achieve spiritual wholeness. This includes embracing the divine poles of masculinity and femininity as expressed through the *sefirot*. Christianity also provides teachings for this via the apocryphal Gospels of Philip and Mary.

Anthropos, Wholeness and the Apocryphal Gospels

The apocryphal gospels are texts that have been hidden or suppressed until recent times. The discovery of the library of Nag Hammadi in Upper Egypt in 1945, along with translations of the Berlin Papyrus and the Rylands Papyrus 463, has helped to piece together these works which include the Gospels of Thomas, Philip and Mary.[21] They provide illumination for the discussion of the Spirit Mate from a Christian perspective that differs from the earlier chapter on the mystics; the messages within the writings, either historical, allegorical or some mix, is closer to the source—

Jesus. These gospels do not currently conform to the canons of the Church, which designate only four Gospels as authoritative scripture, though this rule has been inconsistent.[22] Because they are not accepted, they are not canonical gospels. The Church's Council of Trent in the sixteenth century set the list of accepted scriptures, excluding these, and thereby reinforced an existing power structure, one that rejected women and discredited the power of the feminine.

The dyads continually present in our investigation of the Spirit Mate are the feminine-masculine and the human-divine. The accomplishment of balance in the first propels one into the quest for actualization in the second. This can be gleaned in the brief look at gender and the use of gender transformation to approximate and identify with the deity or the divine.

These ideas are expanded in an examination of the apocryphal Gospels of Philip and Mary. In these texts, the concept of gender is evident as well as the concept of apotheosis. Humankind stands in the center of the creative principles of masculine and feminine, and the words of the Teacher Yeshua, as conveyed through Philip and Mary, provide the spiritual roadmap to actualize the movement from human to god. These steps transform man and woman into the Anthropos, a fully human being and closer approximation of the deity. The living example of this is the relationship between Miriam (Mary) and Yeshua (Jesus).

Briefly, androgyne means both male and female in one being, while anthropos means human being in a general sense. When capitalized, the words take on new meaning, one that bears the connotation of transformation into something greater. For some authors, Anthropos is preferred as a translation for "fully human" over Androgyne because the latter term is somewhat limited to anatomy. This understanding of Anthropos as a different, transformed, full human comes from Logion 114 of the Gospel of Thomas:

Simon Peter said to him: "Let Mary leave us, for women are not fit for the Life." Jesus answered: "See, I have been guiding her so as to make her into a human [Anthropos]. She, too, will become a living breath, like you. Any woman who becomes a human will enter the Kingdom of God."[23]

In the use of Anthropos for fully human, even men must become Anthropi. Women traditionally were not permitted to study Jewish scripture; Mary was stepping beyond the societal bounds (gender culture) in her spiritual study and practice. Yet Jesus, through his relationship with her, is breaking with tradition and guiding her to become 'human' as he also guided Simon Peter. Thus, both men and women can become human, Anthropos, which is the unity of masculine and feminine elements and leads to spiritual progress.

Jean-Yves Leloup is an orthodox theologian who has made the texts of the Gospel of Philip and the Gospel of Mary Magdalene accessible to the modern reader through his translation of the Sahidic Coptic and accompanying analysis. His examination of the texts provides a foundation for a deeper embrace of the Spirit Mate while offering a framework to reintegrate the feminine into Christian understanding in a way that puts it on balanced footing with the masculine. This includes the apocryphal view of Jesus as a fully human being, one with a sexual body (*soma*), a soul (*psyche*) and a spirit (*nous*), rather than a purely divine being. In accepting Jesus as having a unified nature—human and divine—much of the text of the Gospel of Mary Magdalene becomes clear and informs the Spirit Mate work. For it is in recognizing and appreciating the relationship that Jesus, or Yeshua, had with Miriam (the form of "Mary" used by Leloup to distinguish her from other Marys in the gospels) that the idea of fullness becomes possible in the sense of a balanced feminine-masculine nature and that evolution occurs in the sense of moving from human to divine.

In the Gospel of Mary, the phrase "Those who have ears, let them hear!" is often repeated. The need for an altered perception to access information is thereby acknowledged. The disciples, hearing this from a woman's lips, are annoyed, but that only underscores the deeper meaning. Miriam is giving witness to "a different mode of understanding that the masculine mind typically overlooks: a domain…that partakes of the feminine principle."[24] This perception of spirit stands outside ordinary reality. According to Leloup, this is the *imaginal* perception of Henri Corbin (recall Chapter Four), or, as posited here, the shamanic vision of non-ordinary reality. When the reality of this perception is accepted—this middle realm between visionary and intuitive—there is an awakening to "an experience and a knowledge in which the Christ is offered as contemplation, as the archetype of synthesis that the soul of desire seeks to embrace."[25] Upon this embrace, Miriam becomes an *Anthropos* or whole human being, inwardly and outwardly, spirit and body—a product of synthesis. This is the genesis of the double perception of spirit and body.

For those of us working in the shamanic realm, this is confirmation that the Shamanic State of Consciousness[26] is important to this work and that perception within the cosmic zones can bring us valuable and valid experience and knowledge. This experience and knowledge form steps that, through the help of compassionate spirits, move the seeker toward a wholeness and synthesis of the dyads, masculine-feminine and human-divine. Though we may never become fully balanced in masculine and feminine elements, nor achieve actualization of the Anthropos, these are worthy goals and are encouraged through the presence of the Spirit Mate.

The relationship of Yeshua with Miriam serves as a model for the deeper spiritual connection available through this work. Miriam is the special companion of Yeshua. In The Gospel of Philip we learn that: "The companion [*koinonos*] of the Son is Miriam of Magdala. The Teacher loved her more than all the disciples; he often kissed her on the mouth."[27] This kiss has been much debated, but when viewed in the context of Judaism and Gnosticism, it implies breathing together, sharing the same breath. And when the language is considered, nashak (Hebrew for kiss), ruakh (Hebrew for breath), pneuma (Greek for breath) and spiritus (Latin for breath), Yeshua and Miriam "shared the same breath and allowed themselves to be borne by the same spirit."[28] This singular logion, or saying, pulls together the masculine-feminine dyad as well as the human-divine dyad.

The Gospel of Philip uses the language of the bridal chamber to expound on the divine union: "...and the holy of holies is the bridal chamber. Trust and consciousness in the embrace are exalted above all..."[29] The bridal chamber reflects a deeper marriage in which wholeness is the goal. The search for wholeness is born from a sense of *pleroma*, an overflowing toward otherness, rather than a lack, *penia*.[30] This fullness is augmented through relationship with spirit.

While our own quest for a Spirit Mate may be driven from a sense of lack (something is missing), once initiated, a *pleroma* dynamic is set in motion. The more complete we feel or the more fullness we experience through our contact with the other, the more this sense of wholeness translates into ordinary reality. We begin to live from the *pleroma* rather than the *penia*.

From the Workshop Journal: #7

There is power in silence. Silence is something we have difficulty finding even when we are alone. Our thoughts can overpower us, and our minds race on in chatter—out of control and with a life of their own. Noise roars in our ears even behind closed doors. Quieting our thoughts is essential if we are to enter and savor silence. Silence feeds our soul and allows space for newness to arise.

Silence is also important for spiritual development. We all know the person who tells you his or her life story in intimate detail within the first meeting. We blanche and think, "too much information!" Many teachings are expressed as secret teachings based on this principle of silent development.[1] It has been said that speaking of lessons from wise ones, especially our Teachers and Power Animals, can diffuse the power encapsulated in the message.

Journal

Do you include time to be silent daily?

How do you respect your silence and the silence of others?

Minding your words and minding silence are important boundary disciplines. How disciplined are you when it comes to silence? There's an adage that goes something like this: "If you don't understand my silence, how can you understand my words?"

What does this mean to you?

How does this work in the context of a relationship?

In some traditions, being still is a form of prayer. On Mount Athos, the Orthodox monks begin their practice of stillness with these three initial steps: 1) meditate like a mountain, 2) meditate like a poppy, and 3) meditate like the ocean.[2]

— Journal

Sit in silence for three separate periods of time. Set a timer for 20 minutes so that you will know that there is an outer limit to the exercise. For the first period, sit like a mountain. For the next, sit like a poppy. For the final, sit like the ocean. After each take note of the quality of silence you experience. Feel free to repeat these periods as often as you would like and increase the time if you choose.

What is it like to allow yourself silence in these ways?

❋ Journey

Journey to your Teacher and ask why silence is important.

❋ Journey

Journey with your Power Animal on three separate occasions, once each, to a mountain, a poppy and the ocean. Ask each about silence and how they can support you in holding it.

— Journal

Now that you have looked at silence and stillness, is there a difference between the two?

Reel Life: Spirit Mates in Popular Culture: #1

The phenomenon of the Spirit Mate has been present in our popular culture for decades, in song, books and movies. What Baby Boomer can forget the haunting words of singer Bobby Darin's *Dream Lover,*[1] alluding to a perfect love beyond the ordinary realm? Just a year before Bobby's song was released, The Everly Brothers, Don and Phil, recorded another song of pining for a dream lover, a perfect mate (a role which perhaps only the Spirit Mate can fulfill), in their hit *All I Have to Do is Dream:*[2]

Prior to the release of these late 50s songs, a picture of flesh and blood humans interacting with spirit lovers/spirit mates was delivered to the broad American public via cinema. In 1947 Columbia Pictures released *Down To Earth*, starring the screen goddess Rita Hayworth at the peak of her physical beauty; Larry Parks, whose career would later be virtually ended by the Joe McCarthy witch hunt; and some fine (old pro) character actors, such as Edward Everett Horton. The film deals with the Greek goddess of dance and the dramatic chorus known as Terpsichore. In this vivid Technicolor movie, she decides that she must journey down to Earth to change a Broadway musical dealing with the Nine Muses which, in her eyes, is disrespectful and a gross misrepresentation. She determines that this can be accomplished through persuading the show's director, played by Parks, to assign the role of Terpsichore to her and cause him to fall in love with her: easy tasks for a beautiful and talented goddess. Not realizing the literal truth of his words, Danny Miller, the musical's director, says, "I needed a goddess, and a goddess comes down out of nowhere." Later, he tells Terpsichore, "It's almost like you came from another world." And, "A dream is what you are."

Terpsichore's changes to the musical are highbrow and classical and critically ruinous as it goes through its pre-Broadway run. Terp's mentor in heaven, Mr. Jordan (whom we first met in the 1941 movie, *Here Comes Mr. Jordan*, later remade as *Heaven Can Wait*), shows her the vital importance of the musical's success. Terpsichore realizes that her motivation all along has been to change the show, not help Danny, whose very life, she learns, is at stake. Along with this realization comes her awareness that she truly cares for Danny. In fact, Danny loves Terpsichore, and Terpsichore loves Danny. The finished version of the musical, an amalgam of her ideas and Danny's, is a smashing success.

Terp's real mission was to save Danny's life. The success of the musical ensures Danny's survival. Now that his safety is assured, Terpsichore must return to Heaven. She momentarily resists because of her love for Danny and, as a song from the musical states, "People have more fun than anyone." She wants to express her grief through tears, but can't. Mr. Jordan tells her, "Tears are only for mortals; it's the advantage they have over us." Suffice to say that the movie ends happily with the thought that "the spirit never ages."

There are several classical Spirit Mate elements in the story. There is an Upper World, or Heaven, and a Middle World, or physical world. The Spirit Mate, who dwells in the upper realm, wishes to interact with a physical being and provides support and promotes change within that person. The element of love, and certainly sexual attraction, is strongly present and is a prime motivator. The physical being is aware at some level that his partner is a powerful spirit/goddess. The delineation between spirit and the physical is painfully clear.

Chapter 8

Dreamers & Daimons

"My relationship with my Spirit Mate deepened with each meeting with her. In one shamanic journey to her, she invited me into her body so that I could view the world through her eyes. I experienced a sensation of tremendous well-being. My perception was that all my true needs would be taken care of. I would be provided for, there was nothing to worry about, there was only life to be lived and one's earthly mission to be performed."

— from the author's journal, July 1995 (DR)

Two modern authors, Stephen Aizenstat and Caitlín Matthews, illuminate the landscape of the soul by naming and employing a relationship with a being varyingly called Eros or the *daimon*. While the encounters with this being are not strictly shamanic, there are similarities in the discovery and the establishment of active relationship with the Other. Both authors use the contrasexual Other to refine an understanding of the self.[1] Some of the literature (e.g. mythology) referred to in our study thus far has come from distant lands and has perhaps at times seemed remote and somewhat alien. Aizenstat's and Matthews' work arises closer to home in time and place, and is highly accessible and useful to those specifically engaged in shamanic practice. In addition, the material has proven helpful to anyone who wants to understand, expand and explore the fullness of the self as it expresses through relationship and creative gifts. With the guiding hand of Eros, the *daimon/muse,* or Spirit Mate, in place, the human counterpart can tap into the wisdom of the Other and bring it to ordinary reality.

Dream Tending

Parallels can be drawn between the world of the psychologist and the world of the shaman. In his book *Dream Tending,* Stephen Aizenstat, a clinical psychologist, uses the dream and the character of the dream Lover to explore issues in a client's interpersonal relationships. This use of the dream as the interface for the exchange of information is familiar to those who practice shamanism.

Dreams and the shamanic journey provide access to information that is normally hidden. Information is revealed in both of these altered states and—after interpretation of the metaphoric language of the dreamer or journeyer—is brought to normal waking awareness. For eons, humans have plumbed the depths of the sleeping dream in an attempt to glean wisdom. Fred Alan Wolf, in his book *The Dreaming Universe,* traces the study of dreams from the dream temples dedicated to Aesculapius[2] through the psychological and physiological works of Freud, Jung, Hobson and McCarley, and arrives at an understanding of the universe as a quantum field of information that may be tapped during sleep.[3]

Robert Moss, a renowned dreamworker, has investigated altered states of consciousness (ASC) and outlines fourteen states distinct from waking consciousness. These include spontaneous sleep dreams, incubated dreams, dream reentry, hypnagogic experiences, daydreams and reveries, creative visualization, meditation, conscious or lucid dreaming, journeying or conscious dream travel, astral projection, interactive dreaming, dreams within dreams, flow states and finally, continuity of awareness.[4] In discussing human fluctuations of consciousness, Moss offers a nod to anthropologist Holger Kalweit, who observed that humans continually fluctuate between subwakeful and hyperconscious states.[5]

Through these researchers, we have a framework that places dreams and the shamanic journey on equal footing as the loci for encounters with spirits and, especially, the Spirit Mate. The journey and the dream are both points along the consciousness continuum where contact can be made. Michael Harner's *Core Shamanic Theory of Dreams* has further supported this connection and emphasized the usefulness of dreams as a source for information and healing.[6] Thus, the discussion circles back to reflect the philosophy and practice in the dream temples of the Greeks wherein individuals sought help and healing from the spirits during sleeping dreams.

In Aizenstat's work, the core principle underlying the dream and dream content is that both are enlivened—that is, made up of animated and interested actors. This recalls the shaman's view that "everything that is is alive."[7] This also reflects the second principle of Harner's theory of dreams: spirits produce dreams.[8] Thus, when a significant other (or a dream actor in that role) appears on the dream stage, Aizenstat affirms that he or she can be engaged and queried for help and information. These periods of interaction, both within and outside of the dream, Aizenstat calls *dream tending*, which can provide valuable insights into the dreamer's relationships. When integrated into the waking life of the dreamer, this knowledge has proven to be healing and transformative to interpersonal relationships, especially the relationship with the dreamer's ordinary reality significant other.

Aizenstat uses dream tending to help couples deal with relationship difficulties. Each of the partners works with dreams individually and collectively. Through his six-step process that includes 'buy-in' for sharing dreams, creating safety and a responsive attitude, witnessing dreams without judgment, finding Eros, tending the Sacred Marriage and honoring the Third Body, Aizenstat works to move couples beyond disdain, rage and pain.[9] Finding Eros intersects with the Spirit Mate work because it is the place where the dream archetype of the Lover is discovered and begins to fill the dreamer with life force and renewal, as does the encounter with the Spirit Mate. Aizenstat says it is important to make the distinction between the dream Lover and flesh and blood lovers. The temptation arises to impose this image of Eros onto the physical Other which, he says, "gives the human [Other] the power of the divine over us."[10] So, the dream Lover is an emissary of the divine, a kind of spirit. When the physical Other behaves in ways that disappoint, it can be tantamount to rejection by Eros and the resulting disillusionment can lead us further astray in our search for love.

Aizenstat's methodology is to name and tend the dream Lover—Eros. "Without developing relationship to this living image within, the return of authentic love, compassion, and intimacy is rarely achieved."[11] In tending the Lover, he warns against fixing Its shape, making It an object of wish fulfillment, or seeing It as a long-lost lover. This is an admonition against projection. Naming and tending the dream Lover is meant to break new ground as a revelatory process. Eros is unveiled over time and may actually appear in repulsive form from time to time; the Lover can challenge expectations of the ideal. To embrace the elusive nature of Eros, and uncover Its nature, Aizenstat encourages drawing, sculpting and writing of or to the Lover. This promotes intimacy with this figure and softens a heart hardened by life's experience.

Once Eros is found, partnership can evolve. This is the time when the Sacred Marriage develops; "images of the authentic masculine and feminine in each of us (regardless of our gender)… come together to form a divine union."[12] Aizenstat reports that forming this inner union can bring well-being into daily life, affect the quality of life with the human partner, and allow for greater self-acceptance. "Even if we're not currently in a relationship, our contact with these immortals of inner life makes a big difference in the quality of our experience."[13]

The final step in Aizenstat's process involves the emergence of another inner figure, one that embodies the relationship of the couple. One couple with whom he worked called this figure, or being, the 'Holder of Love'. In tending this being that Aizenstat refers to as the Third Body, the couple recognized "an invisible presence who supported them as a couple."[14] Through recognition and tending this Third Body, the life of the earthly marriage can hold vitality and sustain passion.

Anima and Animus

Aizenstat's stage involving the Sacred Marriage is highly reminiscent of Jung's work with the anima and animus. Jung, in his efforts to understand the workings of the conscious and unconscious parts of the self, recognized that portions of the self were often hidden from conscious awareness and surfaced in ways that affected the well-being of the individual. He posited that for each person there was a shadow or hidden part of the self that represented the self's opposite sex aspect. Thus, for every man there is a hidden feminine aspect called the anima and for every woman there is a hidden masculine aspect called the animus.[15] This reflects earlier references to the Kybalion in which the feminine and masculine principles were said to be present in all beings. This masculine-feminine interaction can be balanced through shamanic Spirit Mate work.

According to Jung, when the contrasexual aspects of ourselves are resisted, they erupt in ways that may not be in our best interest. The animus relies on power while the anima uses illusion and seduction as weapons.[16] However, when integrated into the personality, a man's consciousness is supported by the gifts of relationship and relatedness from the anima, while the animus provides a woman's consciousness with a capacity for reflection, deliberation, and self-knowledge.[17] While this language might raise a modern eyebrow, we can read between the lines and glean that the capacity of each individual for self-awareness and the ability to choose novel behavioral strategies is much improved with the healthy integration of the anima or animus.

Classical psychology can only carry us so far in the investigation of the Spirit Mate, since the quest is not truly one of psychology but rather one of spirit.[18] We aren't looking to the anima or animus or an archetype as it is psychologically understood. However, it is the internal relationship with the anima or animus that informs relationship, selection and association with all beings, including the spirits. If a person resists the anima or animus, he may choose less than empowering or inspiring relationships. Relationship with the anima or animus will influence who is accorded attention in ordinary and non-ordinary reality. It is important to exercise discernment and choose friendships wisely in all worlds and to honestly evaluate the basis for the association.

Daimons

The Greek word *daimon* means "a spirit who bridges the divine and human state."[19] This is a far cry from St. Paul's use of the word as a signifier for "devils."[20] *Daimon* was an unfortunate choice of word for a host of intermediary beings who were suddenly relegated to the ranks of Satan's minions by many Christians. This unsavory association is still with us today as *daimon* has mutated to *demon* and has limited our access to a goodly portion of the universe—the *daimonic realm*—out of fear or disbelief.

Early Greeks held the belief that each person was born with a personal *daimon* responsible for his destiny.[21] When this idea met with Christianity, the guardian angel came into being and was dogmatized at the Council of Nicaea in 325 AD. These angels had bodies of light and air with exceptional powers of perception and an ability to move at extraordinary speed.[22] In this form, they truly were bridges between the human and divine states. However, through the writings of the mystic Dionysius the Areopagite (6th century), they lost their mixed physical and spiritual form, becoming purely spiritual.[23] Looking back to the work of Henri Corbin and his elucidation of the three means of accessing information, this loss parallels the loss of the imaginal realm and leaves us with only pure spirit and pure physical. According to Patrick Harpur, author of *Daimonic Reality, Understanding Otherworld Encounters,* this forces a choice about them: they are either literally (physically) real or illusory.[24] In fact, they are real and they are not physical.

This didn't fit the orthodox Christian view, and as Christianity spread across Europe, the *daimons* were displaced; and as they were cast out, they were demonized.[25] Further world views impacted the daimonic realm, particularly the "scientific, secular, sceptical"; and the *daimons* weren't even accorded the honor of demonization, but rather were ignored by many as impossible, imaginary and harmless.[26] And finally, they became 'medicalized'. Even Jung lamented that the gods had become diseases.[27]

However, there are still wisdom holders keeping the knowledge of the daimonic realm alive. These are the storytellers—the wise women and men who traverse the liminal areas to bring to light the soul fire our modern age lacks. Caitlín Matthews is one such wisdom holder. She steps away from the fetters of psychology in her eloquent and studied book, *In Search of Woman's Passionate Soul: Revealing the Daimon Lover Within.* Writing from her heart's own experience and her vast knowledge of folklore, shamanism and women's studies, she breathes life into the inner workings of a woman's soul through acknowledging the inner Lover who ignites a woman's passion like an inner fire that feeds sexual desire and creative current.[28] Calling this inner Lover the *daimon* honors the ageless relationship this spirit has with women and distinguishes it from the relationship a man has with his inner Lover, the *muse.*

Matthews circulated a questionnaire to a number of women she acknowledged as particularly creative, querying them about their inner life and asking about the presence of a contrasexual spirit cum Lover. From this pool, fifty-three respondents surfaced and replied that they had experienced an ongoing relationship with a being, a personal *daimon,* which in some cases had been with them for decades. These women were mostly in mid-life and actively involved in creative endeavors. Their soulful responses indicated a rich inner life and an ability to express in an erudite manner. They demonstrated an active awareness of a spirit in contrasexual form who advised, guided and consoled.[29]

From this body of data, Matthews compiled a list of the forms that the *daimon* may take during the course of a woman's life. There are Primal Forms that appear mainly in childhood and often are in the form of an invisible friend, an animal, a toy or a feature of nature. Obstructing Forms appear when girls and women experience guilt and shame arising from a lack of recognition of their own female self. These forms, which can appear attractive or repulsive, take on the appearance of the raptor, the soul-thief, the criminal, the outlaw or the provoker of strife. Girls and women who distrust their own authority find Patriarchal Forms that appear as the critic, the judge, the watcher or the authority figure. Complementary Forms move the adolescent from the star-struck/pin-up phase to a new state of maturity. This mode can appear on a scale from compensatory (with the masculine) to complementary, depending on maturity level, and is seen as lover, partner, beloved or spouse. The final form is the Inspiriting Form that can appear anywhere from childhood on. Here, a balance is struck between the true *daimon* and the authentic self in which the *daimon* is the inspirer, deity, spirit-companion or initiator. When the *daimon* takes on an Inspiriting Form, a Sacred Marriage becomes possible.[30]

Throughout her writing, Matthews provides ways to understand the complexities of a woman's inner workings with her *daimon.* Questions and meditations enable a woman to perceive the form of the *daimon* she has connected to—wittingly or unwittingly. As the nature of the relationship comes to light, a woman can better understand her physical reality relationships and plot a way to a healthier, authentic self with a *daimon* companion at her side to guide, inform and console. As Matthews says, "the daimon is a universally experienced phenomenon appearing individually among women world-wide, with active power to inspire, support and companion them."[31]

Matthews approaches the *daimon* as a mystic. In another book titled *Sophia: Goddess of Wisdom, Bride of God,* she expounds on the idea of mystical identity. The way one identifies with the deity, in this case the *daimon,* is a great spiritual mystery.[32] The unfolding of this mystery helps us to grow and incorporate aspects of our dual nature, that is, the masculine-feminine and human-divine. The mystical or passionate union brings an experience of non-duality in which subsequent moments of "separation from the object of union is never again so separating...[and]...the possibility of sequential ecstasy accompanies all of life's duties—for the simple reason that the object of our love lends its shine to everything we do, think and feel."[33] There is the same possibility available in learning to work with the Spirit Mate.

Matthews' work focuses on women. Yet it can be extrapolated that each of the forms she presents has a counterpart for men—the *muse*—and through folktale and experience we find that men have their own compensatory, complementary and inspired spirit partners.

From the Workshop Journal: #8

The Tarot is a divinatory tool that has been around since the 14th century. The earliest mention of it is in 1332 when a proclamation against its use was issued by King Alfonse XI of Leon and Castile.[1] The Tarot, a deck of seventy-eight cards, is made up of two subgroups of cards: the Major Arcana and the Minor Arcana. The Minor Arcana is reflected in our playing cards today; there are four suits – cups, wands, swords and pentacles. Today we would know them as hearts, clubs, spades and diamonds respectively. A subset of the Minor Arcana is Pip cards, which refer to common feelings and the routine of daily life in a reading.[2] There are forty, and they are numbered one through ten. A second subset is Court, Royal or Person cards. These are the Kings, Queens, Knights and Pages of each suit. There are sixteen and, in a Tarot reading, they typically represent people in the querent's life.[3]

The Major Arcana is the focus in this exercise. It is made up of twenty-two cards, each representing what some have called an 'archetype'. In my journey work with the Tarot, each represented a guidepost on an internal journey, sharing a particular lesson for my growth and understanding.

Each of the cards in the Major Arcana typically features one figure, the Emperor, for example. Other cards may have multiple people featured, but they appear secondary to the main character as in the Death card, where the knight rides over a field of living and dead humans. Two cards, however, feature couples: The Lovers and The Devil.

It isn't necessary to have any experience with the Tarot to work this exercise. Look online for images of The Lovers and The Devil. If you have a Tarot deck, use it.

➤ Journal

Take some time to look at The Lovers. See what objects or symbols are in the card. See where each of the partners is placing his/her attention. Write your thoughts and feelings as if you were each of the characters in the card. Include the angel overseeing the couple.

❀ Journey

Ask your Power Animal to take you into The Lovers card. Ask the lovers to tell you about their relationship and to share with you their wisdom about love.

➤ Journal

Now take some time to look at The Devil. What do you notice about each of the partners? Write as if you were each of the characters in the card. Include the bat-winged, goat-legged being.

❀ Journey

Ask your Power Animal to take you into The Devil card. Ask this couple to tell you their story. What is the wisdom of their chains?

Reel Life: Spirit Mates in Popular Culture: #2

Portrait of Jennie, the movie starring the great Jennifer Jones, Joseph Cotton and Ethel Barrymore, presents a different sort of Spirit Mate relationship. In this luminous movie, Joseph Cotton plays Eben Adams, a struggling artist in New York City whose work is in dire need of inspiration according to gallery owners Matthews and Spinney, the latter played by Ms. Barrymore. The movie opens not with credits but with a narrator quoting Euripides: "Who knoweth if to die be but to live and that which is called life by mortals be but death." He also tells us that "time does not pass but curves around us, past and future at our side forever." The viewer is clearly in store for a different sort of cinematic experience, one in which the realm of the non-ordinary brushes up against the ordinary.

While walking in Central Park on a wintry day, Eben encounters an enchanting teenage girl, Jennie Appleton, Jones' character. He is feeling light-headed, which recalls the altered state of consciousness. Jennie tells Eben that her parents are high-wire performers at Hammerstein's Theater, which we soon learn burned down decades before. She is dressed in old-fashioned clothes. They walk for a time together, she singing a haunting song: "Where I come from nobody knows, and where I am going everyone goes." She plays a wishing game with him, spinning around three times before revealing her wish that Eben will wait for her to grow up so that they will always be together. She says goodbye. At this point in the movie, Eben and the audience at least have the inkling that Jennie is outside of ordinary reality time, that she is aware of other worlds, and that her love for Eben is boundless. Jennie has left her scarf in the park; ultimately the scarf will be a final proof of Jennie's existence.

After some light-hearted interplay between Eben and his Irish friend Gus (played by David Wayne), who helps Eben secure a mural job and meals at an Irish pub, we find our protagonist at the gallery of Matthews and Spinney, showing them a sketch he has drawn of Jennie. Both are impressed. Mr. Matthews remarks, "There's a quality about the girl which reminds me of long ago. There ought to be something timeless about a woman, something eternal…makes you feel you could meet them anywhere and be inspired by them." What a wonderful—and of course unintended—encapsulation of the qualities of a female Spirit Mate. Eben receives the great sum of $25 for his sketch.

Again, Eben returns to Central Park, this time to the skating pond. The tall buildings bordering the park seem like cathedrals reaching for the heavens. Jennie emerges from the light of the sun on skates. Eben exclaims, "I can't believe it's you. You've grown so." She replies, "Of course I have. Don't you remember my wish?" Their conversation over hot chocolate reveals more non-ordinary aspects of Jennie's life and her elusory nature. Eben tells Jennie that he wants to paint her portrait.

Jennie will find Eben several more times in the course of the film; each time Jennie has matured physically and emotionally well beyond the passage of ordinary reality time. In the meantime, Eben discovers that Hammerstein's Theater burned down in 1910 and that Jennie's parents died in a high-wire accident. Reminiscent of the shaman's experiences outside of time, he walks through the park again, feeling "conscious of an unaccustomed atmosphere, as though time were melting with the snow." He finds Jennie sitting on a bench, weeping over the deaths of her parents, weeping for herself as well. She tells Eben, "Maybe I will always be lonely, but I don't think so, because I am hurrying." So Eben's Spirit Mate admits that she has a great need, the need for his love. She has already provided for his need, the inspiration of the muse. This spirit is not all knowing. She tells Eben that she is going to a convent for schooling and asks him to continue to wait for her.

Later, Eben discusses Jennie with Miss Spinney. Spinney's role as the wise crone is cemented as she says, "As you grow older, you'll learn to believe in lots of things you can't see." He returns to his

apartment, where he finds Jennie looking at his work. Although her portrait is unfinished, we understand the amazing effect that Jennie has had on his painting. She looks radiant on the canvas in her white school dress. She tells him that she is not ready for marriage yet, but feels that they will be together forever. Eben travels to the convent at Jennie's invitation. Once again, she seems to come out of the light. From the balcony of the church, they observe a graduation ceremony in which some of her classmates take the veil and become nuns, the brides of Christ. Here the film sanctions a kind of Spirit Mate relationship.

Eben returns to the city. Swinney and Matthews are shown the portrait of Jennie and are amazed. Matthews comments, "Well, Eben, you found what you were looking for." Eben thinks that "he was caught by an enchantment beyond time and change." While strolling through Central Park at night, Eben sees Jennie running toward him. She says that she has graduated from college and must spend the summer with her aunt on Cape Cod; the audience has been given a sense of foreboding about that area through Jennie's reactions to his paintings of Land's End lighthouse and the sea. They spend the night together walking around New York. She tells Eben, "We were meant for each other. The strands of our lives are woven together and neither the world nor time can tear them apart." They go to his apartment where he finishes her portrait. She tells him that she thinks the painting will make him famous.

Eben longs for Jennie's company through the summer. Eben's friend Gus suggests that they drive to the convent to ask about Jennie. Eben has the feeling that "he is not alone, a feeling that Jennie and I and the world were one…We found beauty together and we could never lose it." This certainly recalls the power of union with the Spirit Mate, which flows into the sense of oneness with all. In the beginning of the movie, before the drama unfolds, the narrator also quotes Keats: "Beauty is truth, truth beauty. That is all ye know on earth, and all ye need to know." And so the Spirit Mate leads one to truth.

At the convent, Eben finds Jennie's favorite teacher, Sister Mary, and asks her where Jennie can be found. "Why, Jennie died, years ago." She reads part of a letter written by Jennie in Cape Cod: "I know the world is so beautiful, but I'm afraid I will never find someone to love me." Sister Mary tells Eben that Jennie used to sail out to a lighthouse. A great tidal wave struck New England at that time, she recalls. Jennie died in the storm.

It is October 4th. Eben has been told that Jennie died on October 5th. He travels to Cape Cod, rents a boat and sails out to the lighthouse, the Land's End Lighthouse, hoping to find Jennie and save her. The film's color changes from black and white to an ominous green as the storm gathers force. Eben's boat crashes on the rocks surrounding the lighthouse. He ascends the spiral staircase of the structure, searching for Jennie. Looking from aloft, he sees a boat, Jenny's sailboat. He races down the spiral. She is on the rocks. He runs to her. They embrace. He is desperate to save her from the gathering wave. She knows her fate and says, "We have all eternity to be together"—the eternal nature of the Spirit Mate relationship and love. "There is no life until you love and have been loved; then there is no death." Eben replies, "it is you I want, not just dreams of you," revealing the pain of the separation of ordinary reality and the world of spirit.

The great wave takes Jennie away, but not before she tells Eben, "We were lonely, unloved. Time made an error; now we're just beginning." Jennie, the Spirit Mate, has a great understanding of love, of the nature of reality, and the nature of death and eternity.

The color of the film turns to sepia, and we find Eben being tended after his rescue from the lighthouse. Swinney is at his side and asks, "You saw her, didn't you?" She holds a scarf on her lap, Jennie's scarf, that she says was found by his side—a proving that her spirit indeed was manifesting in physical form throughout the

story. Eben replies, "I know that I haven't lost her." The camera takes us to a text stating that all of the work of Eben Adams was inspired after his Portrait of Jennie. Then, the final black and white scene shows three teenage girls, one played by our friend Anne Francis, viewing the portrait in a museum. Anne's character says, "I wonder if she was real." Her friend says, "What does it matter? She was real to him." Swinney, the crone, appears to underscore the lesson. Upon overhearing the conversation, she remarks, "How very wise you are."

Then we, the audience, are made privy to the object of their appreciation and wonder. The portrait fills the screen in vivid Technicolor, glowing with the full flush of life, not shades of black and white. That there are many possibilities beyond the presumed polarities of real or not real is made certain.

There are Spirit Mate themes throughout this wonderful movie. It informs us that there is reciprocity in the relationship between the earth-bound human and the Spirit Mate. In *Portrait of Jennie*, Jennie finds the love she so intensely needs, and Eben finds the inspiration that transforms his art and his very being. Jennie, the Spirit Mate, is not all knowing, but her understanding far surpasses that of her ordinary reality partner. She is able to navigate through time with supernatural grace. Her emotions are just as intense as Eben's. It seems that each Spirit Mate story is unique and instructive for all of us.

Portrait of Jennie schools us in the mysteries of death and the mysteries of spirit, showing us the precious value of a Spirit Mate.

Chapter 9

Dakas & Dakinis

"...Now that you have achieved your own enlightenment,
Work for others..."

— Guru to Yeshe Tsogyel[1]

The idea of masculine-feminine balance and the embodiment of the divine are particularly well-developed in the spirituality of the East. Exploration of Tibetan Buddhism shows these Spirit Mate principles in action via inner and outer relationships. Over recent decades, the flow of information from Tibet and the increasing interest in non-mainstream or non-Western spirituality has helped to bring these teachings into general awareness. All beings benefit from the gifts of these revealed treasures as the practices of the adherents stress service to all sentient beings.

Tibetan Buddhism and Sexuality

It is not within the scope of this book to delve deeply into the practices of Yoga, Tantra, or Buddhism, but rather to outline briefly the facets of these practices that inform our discussion of the Spirit Mate.[2] However, it may be useful to understand the use of the words. The root of the word yoga is *yuj* and means "to bind together." This sense of binding deals with breaking the bonds that unite spirit to the world (detachment), unifying the spirit via self-discipline and ultimately encompasses the union of the human soul with God.[3] There are many kinds and styles of Yoga. Tantra, meaning 'what extends knowledge', is a particular, practical system of Yoga.[4]

Buddhism is a spirituality for transcending the human condition based on knowledge and meditational experience of the yogic type.

Through examination of the practices associated with Tibetan Buddhism, various forms of Yoga, pre-Buddhist and pan-Indian spiritualities, it is clear that sex and sexuality play an important role on the path. "*Maithuna* [coitus as both an act and a rite] was known from Vedic times, but it remained for tantrism to transform it to an instrument of salvation."[5] According to Mircea Eliade, there are two ritual values of sexual union: "(1) conjugal union as a hierogamy, or sacred marriage; (2) orgiastic sexual union, to the end either of procuring universal fecundity (rain, harvests, flock, women, etc.) or of creating a 'magical defense.'"[6] Spirit Mate work is concerned with the first, not the second value. Conjugal union, broadly constructed, moves beyond the ordinary marital act to include marriage to a deity. Shternberg says, "the priest attains himself the grace of being the spouse of a deity."[7] Hierogamy can be likewise broadened to include sacred prostitution. Maidens were specifically dedicated to temple sites, "solemnly wedded to a given god…in India and in other places [this] was nothing more or less than *marriage with a god*," and thus a sacred marriage.[8] Through her sexual activities, the hierodule gives pleasure to the deity. Caitlín Matthews clarifies this further by saying, "the Indian *devadasi* and the Mediterranean hierodule have both been misleadingly described as 'sacred prostitutes,' but the sacred service of the body to the divine masculine was at the root of this custom. In this way all men were as the god to the hierodule; and to each male client, the hierodule was the goddess."[9]

In Tibetan Buddhist practice there are two sexual principles at work: *daka,* or male energy, and *dakini,* or female energy. These forms of energy are expressed as *upaya,* skillful means (male) and *prajna* and *sunyata,* respectively profound knowing and emptiness (female). The work of the practitioner is to use the practice of sexual yoga for "opening up further fields of awareness and insight."[10] The initial phases of this practice are intrapersonal and rely upon a relationship with a guru, the taking of particular vows of body, mind and speech, and the invocation of various deities for help in overcoming the illusions of the ordinary world. This idea of sex in the initial stages is consistent with the Kybalionic principle of balancing the masculine and feminine principles within oneself. Through this balance, one can grow and contribute to society. "Whether or not sexual congress is a part of tantric practice, it is the essential genius of Tantra that the most basic and most powerful of human instincts is used as a skilful means to stimulate, or expand, awareness and create insight into the nature of reality, and to generate the will to selfless service."[11]

Assisting the novice in this effort to expand awareness and move to selfless service are the points of refuge or reference that guide the novice's course. The first three are the Three Jewels: the Buddha as the primary example and giver of teachings; Dharma, the body of the Buddha's teachings; and the Sangha, the community of practitioners. Just as important for the Tibetans are the Three Roots, three additional refuges: the Guru, the personal teacher who bestows blessings; the Deva, a deity who transmits power; and the Dakini, a wonderful mix of being and active principle who accomplishes the Buddha's karma. In the Tibetan language the Three Roots are called the Lama, Yidam and Khandro. According to Tsultrim Allione, the Guru is the most important, for it is the Guru who empowers a practice and, through his presence, facilitates a path to greater and deeper levels of awareness. The "Lama's pronouncements and precepts are the dharma, and his word assumes the sanctity of absolute truth."[12] It is the presence of the Guru which keeps the neophyte from getting ahead of himself and from engaging in unsuitable practices.

There are three levels of practice for the practitioner, who is sometimes called a tantrika, a yogin or yogini. At the first level, the deity is invoked and visualized in front of the practitioner. The tantrika merges with the deity while reciting the deity's specific mantra or sound formula. This is the Outer Practice. At the second level, the tantrika works with the deity through the activation of the subtle anatomy of nerves, breath and essence. This is the Inner Practice. The third level, called the Secret Practice, brings the practitioner into direct contact with the deity's principle.[13] These are the steps for ever closer identification with the divine for the purpose of awakening awareness and for reaching beyond the limits of human existence. This resembles Spirit Mate work in that it, too, calls for identification with a spirit being for the purpose of expansion and evolution.

These practices can become sexualized as part of an empowerment process. The empowerments are a form of transmission from the Guru to the disciple and are four in number, each serving a specific purpose for the initiand. The first is the Vase Initiation. At this stage, the novice becomes empowered to practice mahayoga, the creative process of meditation.[14] It is also the phase in which the body is purified.[15] The second empowerment is the Mystic Initiation. This empowers the practice of anuyoga, which stimulates the field with pure vibration, sound and energy.[16] While the nature of the Vase Initiation is somewhat serene and peaceful, this initiation is charged with ferocity. A level of illuminated communication is activated, opening a superior field of energy.[17] The third initiation is the Wisdom Initiation, in which blocked forms are broken loose. It is the place where empty, essential being can be experienced and the level where sexual practices are introduced for the circulation of *prana* ("breath" in Sanskrit) and to further open awareness.[18] The final empowerment is the Word Initiation. This empowers the yogin and yogini to practice Dzogchen atiyoga, the highest tantric path.[19] It is the simultaneous realization of the first three empowerments.[20]

Throughout these initiations and practices both the masculine (daka) and feminine (dakini) principles, or deities, are activated. This is done through visualization, in which practitioners see themselves as merged with the deities. The deities themselves are often represented in the classic yab-yam posture: the male emanation of the deity large and formidable, while the female aspect is smaller, coiled about him in an embrace. This is the partnership of *upaya* with *prajna* and *sunyata*. The gods have their consorts and the practitioner, through the act of identification with the deities, also has a consort—the deity. This is the first phase of 'spirit mating' that initiates a move toward the balance of the masculine and feminine polarities and a shift toward non-dualism or wholeness. As Tsultrim Allione has said about these images and their use to stimulate union, not only with the deities but internally: " [these images are] sexual and spiritual, ecstatic and intelligent, wrathful and peaceful."[21] This reminds us that as humans we are multi-faceted, and wholeness is achieved only when we establish healthy relationships with all aspects of ourselves. Here is an echo of Matthews' work with the *daimon;* when we are imbalanced or immature in relationship to certain parts of ourselves, we attract daimons that reflect that imbalance. Thus, the goal in work with the deities is to seek a new balance built on wholeness.

Yeshe Tsogyel – The Dakini

Yeshe Tsogyel is one of the most famous women in Tibet. The book *Sky Dancer: The Secret Life and Songs of the Tibetan Lady Yeshe Tsogyel* traces her spiritual journey as she perseveres to her ultimate goal of her reality becoming "primal space"—that is, to achieve Buddhahood in one lifetime.[22]

Her birth was marked by many auspicious signs, and it was clear that her origins were divine. Her hair hung to her waist and she sat in a perfect lotus just moments after her birth. Showing her mouth full of perfectly formed teeth, she sang praises to the great sage of Orgyen, the Pure-land of the Dakinis.[23] Within one month she had attained the appearance of an eight year old and was hidden for ten years, after which her beauty was discovered and people traveled for miles for a glimpse of her.

This unusual beginning was the basis for a life peppered with travel and spiritual adventures. Each event, from her marriage to the Emperor to living in self-exile, for example, marked a step along Tsogyel's path to the age of 211, culminating in her attainment of Buddhahood. The relationship she had with Padmasambhava, her Guru, was critical for achieving Buddhahood in one lifetime. Peme Junge (another name for Padmasambhava) joined with the Goddess Sarasvati in the Buddhafield of Sambhogakaya to create the Nirmanakaya emanation which was to become Tsogyel. The story goes on to tell of the many forms or emanations of Tsogyel[24]: she is Kuntuzangmo, or infinite and noble femininity, in the Dharmakaya; the Five-Wisdom Consort in the Sambogakaya; and a multitude of forms (Tara, Sarasvati, a princess, ordinary girl, business woman, prostitute, etc.) in the Nirmanakaya.[25]

Tsogyel turned to Peme Junge as she matured and desired initiations. She was given to him as a gift from her husband Trisong Detsen, the Emperor, so that he could receive initiations. Tsogyel took refuge in the Guru, who made her his Lady Consort and granted her the Vase Initiation, the Mystic Initiation, the Wisdom Initiation and the Word Initiation. Each of these initiations provided an empowerment to Tsogyel that expanded her experience of ordinary reality through contact with the non-ordinary reality of the Guru.

The language of initiation is highly erotic. As with the Christian mystics, there is little other way to describe the currents of energy that are transmitted during the empowerments. At the Vase Initiation, the Guru says, "Now offer your mystic mandala."[26] Tsogyel says that she does so without shame, or in the manner of the world. The Guru, invoking the deity, called light to descend through his body and "his mystical vajra arose in wrath and as Vajra Krodha he united with the serene lotus in absolute harmony."[27] This practice awakened the kundalini energy of Tsogyel, and it rose through her four centers, producing joy, supreme joy, no-joy and spontaneous joy.[28] The Guru told her to prepare to offer the mandala again, which she did, and offered it to him seven times over, delighting the Guru.

Tsogyel requested the next empowerment, the Mystic Initiation. The Guru acquiesced and, with the sound of laughter, granted the empowerment of the Lama's Speech. In this initiation, Tsogyel received the means of identifying with the Guru and his Consort in union as Hayagriva. She reports, "...my own body was transformed into the body of the Vajra Varahi...I intuitively realised the meaning of psychic nerves, energy flows and seed-essence; the five passions were transmuted and manifested as the five modes of Awareness."[29] In this way, Tsogyel was introduced to her own body as a "divine mandala." This recalls the double perception of body and spirit.

After practicing to perfect control over the new awareness, Tsogyel again implored the Guru for yet another empowerment. In full trust she begged for the initiation and the Guru responded, "if you wish the seed to infuse your inner mandala, offer your mandala of mystic delight." And Tsogyel replied, "I anointed my mandala with the five sacred substances, and made further petition: 'Buddha Hero of Pure Pleasure, do as you will. Guru and Lord of pure Pleasure, with true energy and joy, I implore you to inject the seed into the inner mandala. And I will guard the secret of the method with my life.'" The Absolute Heruka (the Guru), "his magnificent flaming vajra in a state of rapacity...took command of the lotus throne" and conferred the empowerment upon her.[30]

After her initiations, the Guru exhorted Tsogyel to find a consort with whom to practice. He told her, "Now, girl, without a consort, a partner of skilful means, there is no way you can experience the mysteries of Tantra."[31] And here is the crux that relates most clearly to the Spirit Mate. "The tantric practices of Tibetan Buddhism concern the embodiment of the deity by the practitioner...tantra brings together living physical consorts who embody the deities within their union and thus enable Wisdom to be manifest to the world."[32] Thus, the two dyads of the Spirit Mate are consolidated. The practice employed to bring masculine-feminine wholeness is based on the human-divine dyad and is an approach to attaining sacred union.

Another dimension of sacred union is revealed through Yeshe Tsogyel. She essentially becomes the Spirit Mate for every initiate into the Nyingma Inner Tantra.[33] In her many *kaya* emanations, she is *the* Dakini, both a being and an activating principle, and she leads the initiand along the path to greater levels of awareness as a consort unifying skilful means with profound knowing and emptiness.

The Dakini is typically represented with three objects: the kartik (hooked knife), the kapala (skull cup) and the khatvanga (three-pronged staff).[34] In relation to the Spirit Mate, the khatvanga is most important. Often called the secret or hidden consort, it represents the cross-gendered energy that must be incorporated into each tantrika—feminine for males and masculine for females. While the tantrika can stand alone, the process of visualizing oneself as the deity (Daka or Dakini) with a khatvanga initiates this incorporation and builds wholeness.[35]

The idea of a hidden consort is reflected in a story about Guru Peme and his consort Yeshe Tsogyel. When they visited King Trisong Detsen, the Guru transformed Tsogyel into a khatvanga to protect her from the king's queen, who harbored ill intentions for the Guru and his Consort. When the king asked the Guru about Tsogyel, the Guru replied that all his actions were instruction and, touching the staff, revealed Tsogyel.[36] The wonder at this action inspired faith within the king's court and plots were set aside.

Once again, shape-shifting is an element of the Spirit Mate. The story echoes the time when Zeus hid Io from Hera in the form of a white cow. Recall, too, the Saorans and the presence of the tutelary focused in the rice pot hanging from the rafters. The *ayami*, as well, can appear as a woman, a tiger or a dragon. Even the *blolo* mate of the Baule can appear in many guises, with the exception of the ordinary reality spouse. The Spirit Mate is ever fluid, shifting and adapting as we ourselves change and grow.

From the Workshop Journal: #9

We can define the ego as the "I" of any person, the conscious part of a person's psyche that deals with the outside world—in Freudian terms, the arbiter between the id (the pleasure seeking part of ourselves) and the superego (where our conscience dwells). There are healthy egos and unhealthy egos. So, how goes your ego? Is it responsible for the things that you accomplish? Is it the reason that you feel separation from all that is? Is it the cause of much misery for you?

— Journal

How would you characterize your ego? What are your ego's positive and negative aspects? What is the advantage to going beyond the ego? How would one do so? What role does your ego play in your relationships?

❀ Journey

Go to your Teacher and ask him/her to expound upon the topic of human ego.

Reel Life: Spirit Mates in Popular Culture: #3

Released in 1947, *The Ghost and Mrs. Muir*, set in England, presents yet another Spirit Mate story. Starring Rex Harrison as the ghost Captain Gregg and Gene Tierney as the widow Mrs. Muir, this superb movie set in 1900 deals with the relationship between a mortal woman and a male spirit.

A year after Mrs. Muir's husband's death, the widow announces to her manipulative in-laws that she intends to move with her young daughter Anna, played by Natalie Wood, her dog and her maid Martha to the coast. She seeks help from a realtor to find a suitable rental. Mr. Coombe reluctantly shows her Gull Cottage, the house she is drawn to—a house that we quickly learn is haunted. Soon after moving in, on a stormy night, Lucy, the widow, senses the presence of the ghost. Captain Gregg reveals himself and tells her that he has been looking after her and comments on how beautiful she is. She replies that she needs no help. However, the themes of Spirit Mate protection and sexual attraction have been established. Harrison's character is headstrong, thorny, and lusty—a contrast from the polite and placid Mrs. Muir.

He tells her that the house is his, that he built it, and intends to stay in it. Wanting him to leave, she ultimately agrees to a compromise— the Captain will limit his presence to her bedroom. He assuages her concern over this startling idea by saying, "Confound it, I'm a spirit. I have no body. All you see is an illusion." The relationship begins to develop. Captain Gregg tells Mrs. Muir that she should stop wearing mourning clothes; anyway, he says, she really didn't love her husband. She sees the truth in his observations. He talks of being a seaman. In light of her economic woes, the Captain proposes that she write a book about his life to be called *Blood and Swash*. He will dictate the book to her. She will call him Daniel; he will call her Lucia, a "proper name for a queen." Addressing her skepticism,

Daniel tells her, "I am real. I'm here because you believe I'm here… keep on believing and I'll always be real for you."

Due to Lucy's inability to pay the rent, an eviction from the cottage becomes a possibility. Fortunately, the book is finally finished. Daniel and Lucia's interactions have promoted an ever-closer relationship. He asks, "What's to become of us?" She replies, "I'm afraid we've got ourselves into an awful fix." He encourages her to be in the world and see men. Lucy takes the manuscript to Mr. Sproule, the publisher recommended by Daniel, who tries to throw her out of his office, but finally, after looking at the manuscript, declares it to be a wonderful tale. At the publishing house, she meets Miles Fairley, played by George Sanders, a flirtatious, romantic and handsome writer of children's books.

An affair begins that the captain objects to, not only because of jealousy, but also because of his concern for her feelings. Finally, while Lucy is asleep, Daniel tells her, "You've chosen life. That is why I am going away. You've been dreaming of a sea captain who haunted this house. In the morning and years after, you'll remember it as a dream."

In the next scene, Lucy receives a letter with a 100-pound advance for her book. She travels into the city to finalize her royalty payments. She decides to visit Miles, whom she plans on marrying, as a surprise. At his home, she meets Miles' wife, who indicates that Lucy is not the first woman to fall prey to Miles' charms! Lucy is overwhelmed with shock and grief. Waves crash upon the rocks to Bernard Hermann's evocative musical score, indicating the passage of time. Lucy reflects on the dreams she had of the captain. Her daughter is now a young woman and brings her fiancé home to meet Lucy. Anna reveals that she had many talks with Captain Gregg until the time when he suddenly disappeared. Anna asks, "Did we have the same dream? Did you fall in love with him, too?" Lucy says, "We made him up. I had the sea and the gulls and my dreams."

More time passes. Lucy is an older woman now, who receives news of her granddaughter's engagement. She sits in her chair drinking a glass of milk brought to her by Martha. She drops the glass and slips slowly from her body in death. Captain Gregg appears and says, "You'll never be tired again." Lucy is young again, radiant, and the two of them, after looking back at Lucy's old body, walk hand in hand down the stairs, through the front door and into the light.

Reel Life - Summing Up

The late 1940s saw numerous movies that featured spirits interacting with mortals. But the three that we have chosen to present in this book focus on romantic relationships between spirits and humans. Summing them up, in *Down to Earth* and *Portrait of Jennie*, the mortal is ultimately aware that the Spirit Mate is real. In *The Ghost and Mrs. Muir* that recognition is sublimated until the point of death. In *Down to Earth* Terpsichore descends to earth for somewhat selfish reasons, asserts her power, helps Danny, and eventually falls in love with him. At the end of the movie, we learn that their love is eternal. In *Portrait of Jennie* the spirit's love for the mortal human is there at the start of the relationship; the mortal's love for Jennie and his acceptance of her realness develop over time. Again, the spirit helps the mortal in his ordinary reality life by inspiring his art, which leads to commercial success. In *The Ghost and Mrs. Muir* a chance confluence of a spirit and mortal results in the mortal being helped (Lucy becomes economically self-sufficient) and a great love developing into an eternal marriage.

Each movie falls short, to varying degrees, of portraying the classic Spirit Mate relationship scenario. Because classically, the relationship is established, it develops and then perpetuates throughout the rest of the mortal's life. Once met, the Spirit Mate is an ally, a teacher, a companion, and a guardian for the mortal. The mortal and the Spirit Mate do not have to wait until the mortal's death to be together.

These movies reveal that the theme of Spirit Mate has seeped into modern culture and continues to be a compelling phenomenon. More recently, *Down to Earth* was the inspiration for the movie *Xanadu* (1980), starring Olivia Newtown-John and Gene Kelly. *Heaven Can Wait* (1978), with Warren Beatty and Julie Christie, certainly has elements of the Spirit Mate phenomenon; and the vastly successful *Ghost* (1990), with Demi Moore and Patrick Swayze, deals with a spirit's unbounded love for his still living wife.

❦ Activity

The films highlighted in our study of the Spirit Mate reflect our passion for old classic movies. We also have a fondness for songs from the 1950s.

Brainstorm to see if you can think of other films or songs that speak to an experience of the Spirit Mate. Discuss which aspects of the Spirit Mate relationship explored in this book also appear in the movie(s) or song(s) you come up with.

Chapter 10

Modern Martyr

"Last night, on retiring, my dear husband was with me as he has not been for some time – I mean, in a different way – and we united sexually. I cannot describe how happy I was to possess and be possessed by him."
— from a note in Ida Craddock's diary about her spirit husband Soph[1]

During the period from 1850 to the early 1900s in the United States, there was a remarkable confluence of spiritual ideas that became a fertile brew for one particular woman: Ida Craddock. Often called the Third Great Awakening, it was a time when 'modern' people were exploring the boundary of life and death through Spiritualism, a belief system that burst on the scene in 1848 with attendant knocks, raps and voices from beyond the grave. The powers of the mind were being prospected for 'magnetism', and how-to books were written on its use. Communities exploring novel ways to live and relate, like the Oneida Community in Upstate New York, were established as living experiments of new ideas. In the midst of this storm of spiritual activity, women were rebelling against patriarchy and speaking out as suffragettes.

Craddock was a woman before her time. She was a scholar, a suffragette and an outspoken advocate for sexual education. During her life (1857–1902), Ida railed against social problems in places like Philadelphia, Chicago, Washington, DC and New York—cities where she lived and gave counsel on sexual matters. She was sensitive to the "toll exacted by repeated childbearing on the health of women of the time, as well as the social problems created by having more children than a family could support. Maternal and infant mortality rates were extremely high in the late 19th century," and Ida felt bound to do something about these conditions.[2]

Ida Craddock was passionate in distributing her forthright sexual education pamphlets and stood toe-to-toe against Anthony Comstock, a congressman and bully, who used the law regarding sending "obscene, lewd, or lascivious" materials through the mail to have Ida convicted and sent to prison. This material included information about "contraceptive devices and any information concerning sex, birth control, or abortion."[3] Congressman Comstock was also a voluntary postal inspector who sought out "objectionable" material in order to suppress it, and the law he enforced—the Comstock Law—is still on the books today.[4] He, too, was a product of his time. For while New Thought and other more liberal philosophies were taking hold, society also embraced ideas of social purity and clean living. Organizations such as the Young Men's Christian Association and the Women's Christian Temperance Union arose—both with "political agendas that called for the prohibition of alcohol and the regulation of sexual behavior."[5] Comstock founded the New York Society for the Suppression of Vice, "a private moral enforcement squad that was spun off from the YMCA."[6] Comstock attempted to suppress Ida over the years and finally succeeded, using a kind of entrapment through a letter (allegedly from a minor) requesting Ida's pamphlets. Suspecting a trap, Ida responded negatively to the request. Unfortunately, this didn't deter Comstock, who secured a conviction against her with a judge sympathetic to his cause. Ida was prevented from making an adequate defense and was convicted according to laws regarding indecency and that which is "harmful to minors."

Yet, in spite of the conviction and regardless of the wall of adversity, Ida Craddock refused to crumble. She proved her bravery against the system by repeatedly moving to avoid her mother, who wanted to confine her to an asylum for her activities, and Comstock, who wanted to make an example of her. While intermittently supporting herself as a stenographer, typing teacher and research assistant, she wrote about things sexual with an aim to improving society's lot. Her first treatise, *The Danse du Ventre (1893)*, was written in response to an outcry about belly dancers at the 1893 World's Fair held in Chicago.[7] Criticized by Comstock and others as inappropriate, the dance was defended by Ida as "a religious memorial of a worship which existed thousands of years ago all over the world, and which taught self-control and purity of life as they have never been taught since."[8] Her essay, published in the *Chicago Clinic*, a medical journal, related the dance to the sexual relationship between a husband and a wife and suggested that "the divine power who rules the world requires from us all, not asceticism, but self-controlled and pleasurable use of *every* passion in His service."[9] Making certain that her remarks as a single woman were considered credible, in the last paragraph of the monograph Craddock disclosed that she could speak from the standpoint of a wife. "My husband, however, is in the world beyond the grave, and had been there for many years previous to our union, which took place in October, 1892. In accordance with angelic laws, he can come clearly to me when I keep the way of right living and clear thinking."[10]

After the publication of the *Danse du Ventre*, there was a furor over her disclosure. A colleague and suspected former lover refuted her claim before the Ladies' Liberal League. Ida's mother wanted to commit her. Hurt and betrayed, Ida fled to London to act as research assistant to W. T. Stead, a British journalist and Spiritualist she had met while he was in New York on business. In London, Ida worked at the offices of *Borderland*, Stead's Spiritualist journal, and had time to conduct her own research in *Borderland's* library and the British Museum. The result of her efforts was her *Heavenly Bridegrooms (1894)*, which was a defense of her spiritual marriage, citing Biblical and historic precedence for the relationship. It may be tempting to dismiss this work as an elaborate means to conceal Ida's 'illicit' physical sexual relationships; her first biographer conjectures that she may have had two such ordinary contacts. Ida's "diaries of her spiritual experiences from the spring of 1894 until the end of her life" are very detailed and contain full conversations with discarnate beings, including Soph, her spirit husband, and are completely compelling.[11]

In *Heavenly Bridegrooms,* Ida opens with, "It has been my high privilege to have some practical experience as the earthly wife of an angel from the unseen world."[12] Through the rest of her essay she presents many references to texts which argue for the presence of angels engaged in sexual relations with earthly women. She used Scripture to prove that these angels are not demonic and that "clear thinking on the part of every would-be occultist" is critical for accuracy in the mediumship required to communicate beyond the grave.[13] She covers such things as spirit children and the changing nature and appearance of the spirit husband. She also adds a reason for ordinary reality wedlock; it is not only for procreation but also for an exchange of strength and happiness.

Ida composed several other pieces dealing with sexual relations. Her greatest was *The Marriage Relation (1900),* a work of some 437 pages. It was written in Denver where she recovered from a trial in which she was convicted for sending one of her pamphlets through the mail and received a three month suspended sentence. Her other works are: *Psychic Wedlock (1895), Right Marital Living (1899),* and *The Wedding Night (1900).* In all of these, Ida worked out what she called her system of sexual mysticism, which had three distinct degrees.

"The first degree, which she called 'Alpha-ism,' required strict sexual abstinence, the only permitted exception being for the purpose of procreation."[14] The term Alpha-ism was probably derived from E. B. Foote's 1882 book *Dr. Foote's Replies to the Alphites.* Foote was one of Ida's protectors, a Freethinker, who, through his book, was responding to a journal called *The Alpha,* which promoted sex only for the purpose of procreation. Stepping beyond the Christian dictates dominating the times, Ida's first degree calls to mind the initial steps on the path of the tantrika. The early initiations deal with self-purification, and as the previous chapter (Dakas & Dakinis) indicates, sexualization of practice wasn't included until the third, or Wisdom Initiation, since the initiand hadn't yet moved to equanimity regarding emotions.

The second degree, referred to as *Diana,* permitted sexual intercourse, but without ejaculation on the part of the male. This, too, calls to mind the training of the male in various yogic practices in which the "adept becomes able to control his semen as he controls his breaths…'immobilization' of the semen through *pranayama* is always connected with a similar immobilization of the states of consciousness."[15] The use of the term 'Diana' was cited in Ida's *Heavenly Bridegrooms* and was also the name for the male continence practice employed at the Oneida Community.

Ida's third degree involved "inviting God to become a mystical third partner in a couple's lovemaking, thus providing them with access to divine consciousness."[16] This degree was most probably influenced by Asian thought. During a walk in London's Kensington Gardens, Ida conversed with a Mr. Harte, who shared with her "the Hindu idea that a god can enjoy only through a mortal, and that mortals ought to share their delights with the gods, or with God."[17] Once again there are echoes of Tibetan practice, in that earthly consorts, each merged with a cross-gendered deity, provide intercourse for their partner with the divine. Also, it was very likely that Ida had been inspired by *Raja Yoga* by Vivekananda, a book that was "sweeping the nation in popularity," so much so that she "established the Church of Yoga with herself as 'pastor and priestess.'"[18]

Ida Craddock was a woman inspired by her ideals and used her relationship with her angel husband to forward her cause. Unfortunately, the power of the patriarchy, personified by Anthony Comstock, pushed her beyond the limit of endurance, and she took her life on October 17, 1902. She left two letters, one to her mother and one to *The Truth Seeker* newspaper, explaining her actions and giving voice to a defense that she had been unable to present at her second and final trial. Rather than face a term of impossible incarceration, she killed herself in the early hours on the day of her sentencing. Her actions were viewed as a kind of martyrdom and the outcry marked the beginning of Comstock's loss of power and influence.

One of the things that makes Ida and her Spirit Mate relationship so interesting, beyond her disclosure of it to the public, is that it made an impression upon Aleister Crowley. In 1914, Crowley, the head of the British Ordo Templi Orientis (O.T.O.), met with Ida's first biographer, Theodore Schroeder, a Free Speech lawyer, during a visit to New York. In 1919, a "glowing review of *Heavenly Bridegrooms* for his occult periodical *The Equinox*" appeared with one of Crowley's most famous quotes: "When you have proved that God is merely a name for the sex instinct, it appears to me not far to the perception that the sex instinct is God."[19]

There are distinct differences between *sexual mysticism* and *sexual magic,* which was developed in part by Crowley. Ida was a mystic interested in the use of her sexual relationship with her angelic husband to approach the divine and to reciprocate the pleasures of her life to the divine. This is very different from the use of sexual energy to develop powers, or the use of power akin to the idea of 'magnetism', exerting influence over others or using them for one's own ends. There is guidance in this from Tibetan Buddhism. Through practice, it is possible to develop magic powers called 'ordinary *siddhis*'. "These are the powers that come as signs of progress in meditation practice. Although they are extraordinary from the point of view of the world, they are called ordinary to make it clear that these powers are not the real point of doing the practice...the real point is to go beyond attachment and return to the primordially pure state of wisdom."[20] This attitude is reflected in the work of Ida Craddock.

From the Workshop Journal: #10

The ego can get in the way of relationships. Problems arising from the ego are sometimes labeled and grouped in the following ways:

- The three fundamental poisons: passion, aggression, ignorance.[1]
- The five poisons: ignorance, attachment, anger, jealousy, pride.[2]
- The seven deadly sins: pride, envy, gluttony, lust, anger, greed, sloth.[3]
- The seven po: anger, desire, fear, joy, grief, love, hatred.[4]

～ Journal

How would you define each of the above? How might each be a problem or a challenge in a relationship?

～ Journal

If you had a wise advisor, what would that advisor tell you about each of the poisons, sins or po? Write a short paragraph of caution from this advisor. Include details of specific relationships where the poison, sin or po is active.

✸ Journey

Ask your Power Animal to take you to a representative of each of the five poisons. Do this one journey at a time. Ask the representative two questions: What is the lesson you have for me? What is the gift that can come to me through this understanding?

Each of the poisons and each of the sins have a counterpart that operates as its polar opposite. For example, humility is said to be the counterpart of pride; kindness, envy; abstinence, gluttony; chastity, lust; patience, anger; liberality, greed; diligence, sloth.[5]

— Journal

How do you define these counterparts? Are these counterparts gifts or the same challenge, in another form?

— Journal

Write about the gift and challenge of the counterpart.

❋ Journey

Ask your Teacher for a way to create balance between each poison and its counterpart. Again, one poison per journey.

From the Workshop Journal: #11

Joseph Campbell advised us to follow our bliss. Yet many follow their poison, and the planet and its inhabitants suffer. What is bliss?[1] *Webster* tells us that it is "supreme happiness, utter joy."

— Journal

How many people do you know who are following their bliss?
Is bliss worth pursing at all?
Do humans deserve bliss, considering the state of our planet and the devastation that we have wrought upon our Mother Earth?

Mental attitude is a strong determinant of physical health and longevity. According to a comprehensive study found in the journal *Applied Psychology: Health and Well-Being*, happiness clearly promotes a longer life and a healthier body.[2] Over 160 individual studies were considered. One study followed 5000 college students over 40 years—the optimists outlived the pessimists. Clearly, bliss is desirable if you want to live a long life and be healthy in the process.

— Journal

Consider the following questions. What makes you happy? Are you doing what makes you happy? If so, how often? Do you accept mediocrity - or worse - when it comes to friendship, work, avocation, diet, etc.? If you were granted five wishes for your life, what would they be? How can you bring these things into your life?

✺ Journey

Ask your Teacher how best to achieve bliss.

It's been said that a key to a joyful life is gratitude. When we give and receive gratitude, we are reminded of the many blessings that flow in our lives. Want to fuel your bliss? Express gratitude.[3]

Journal

Every night before going to sleep, make a list of ten things for which you are grateful. If you're having a hard time of it, prime the pump with basics like the ability to breathe, the ability to read this book, the ability to think. In the morning upon waking, take a moment to be grateful for the gifts the day is bringing.

Activity

Maintain an awareness of gratitude throughout a given day and see how your day goes. Try being an unforgiving grouch the next day and see how it goes. The contents of your life might not change, but your attitude shifts. Which feels better?

Chapter 11

The Experience[1]

"In another journey, my Spirit Mate asked me to be particularly observant and to look for the magic that is always in the world. I learned that this is a way of slowing down time and for finding satisfaction in everyday life."
— from the author's journal, July 1995 (DR)

The Spirit Mate Workshop promotes the exploration of love and loving relationships. The greatest concern for most participants in the workshops has been their ability to meet the Spirit Mate. While it must be said that some participants arrive at a workshop already aware of the identity of a Spirit Mate and seek reassurance and validation that their experiences are real, most are genuinely curious and want to connect with one and see what happens. Some people meet a Spirit Mate in their initial journeys, even during an introductory workshop, and are confused about their experiences, largely due to the sexual component. Our role has been to support these encounters with the Spirit Mate and to help people integrate their non-ordinary experiences into their ordinary reality lives.

When one initiates a spiritual quest—this includes signing up for a workshop—the spirits can begin opening pathways. It is as if the asking or seeking prompts a response. It happened this way for one student.

I became aware that my Spirit Mate was very ready and excited to be finally making the connection in the week prior to the workshop. I began to feel a presence around me during that week, and my dog would very often gaze at something in the room, and then come curl up near me as he continued to gaze at one spot. After a few days of this, I journeyed and was told it was my Spirit Mate hovering very close by; he did not want to be missed. I asked him, via my Power Animal, to not be so present as it was scaring both me and my dog, and the strong presence faded a bit. But it didn't leave. He said later that he had been waiting for me since I was two years old, that he "followed my energy signature" to my Ordinary Reality body. And he had waited patiently until he could be recognized by me. —K.D.

In our Spirit Mate Workshops, work typically begins with already established allies. The Teacher and the Power Animals are wise advisors whose counsel is used in meeting the Spirit Mate. This underscores the importance of well-established relationships with these two primary shamanic allies. They are the first line of discernment in working with the spirit worlds; working with them promotes a strong sense of self. While the strength and clarity of our intention guides our experiences, it is reassuring to know that the Power Animal and Teacher stand ready to assist and protect.

I was told that I would meet my Spirit Mate in the Upper World on the next day, but was not given any other details concerning this meeting. The next day my Power Animal took me to a new area of the Upper World. I saw men with masks emerging from the woods saying, "Hi, ____," as they walked by, but I felt nothing as they passed me. I was thirsty and knelt down to get water for my Power Animal and me and saw this amazing reflection in the water of a man in a mask. My entire body experienced enormous amounts of heat when I saw him. I turned to him and said, "Hi, I'm ___," and he said, "I know." A deep peaceful feeling fell over my entire being as we walked toward a clearing. Suddenly a group of drummers and other people appeared. I asked if he were my Spirit Mate, and he said yes. Then I inquired about what he did and learned that he was a shaman in a nearby village. The drummers started playing, and we danced until the drumming ended. His mask was red and purple with intricate designs, but he would not remove it until our next journey. —Anonymous

Spirit Mates can be companions, consorts, teachers. They may be guides, lovers or angels. They may wear peaceful or wrathful guises. In using the help of our allies to discover them, we exercise trust and begin to explore the possibilities of relationship with a Spirit Mate.

Right after meeting [me], my Spirit Mate gave me perspective and advice on my relationship with my mother. This was probably the most important thing he has helped with, aside from what he has tried to tell me about my relationship with myself. —L.V.

Spirit Mates can also be shape-shifters. They can change their non-ordinary reality identity to provide opportunities for us to learn. One student shared that his relationship with his Spirit Mate had multiple components—helping, sexual and spiritual. In his experience, the Spirit Mate transformed herself and him at various times in order to teach him about the roles of male and female energy in what he calls the Spiritual Energy Web. Other students report the following.

I met her very early on and wasn't sure what was happening at the time, but just went with it. There were moments when I felt a bit queasy when things started to become clear. The sex part of it got...wild. There was a strong sense that she was appearing to me as I needed her to appear to me; and when I refused that, out of some prideful need to see "reality," she took me just far enough in to give me the shudders. Love and sexual expression took on an eternally simultaneous transgressive/ redemptive aspect. —Shadi

My spirit mate appears most often as a large rank-smelling Bear who lives and dens in the mountains... Most often he is male but sometimes female and sometimes appears in many different emanations, for example, sometimes a huge tall shadowy spirit like a deva or upper world spirit. When I met him in non-ordinary reality for the first time, he said, "Come marry me, you are old now, you would not have to worry about having half-bear offspring." In the very beginning of our relationship, for example, during the workshop, I worried about having an inter-species relationship with a non-human spirit, but that concern quickly dissipated. —Anonymous

Sometimes the learning is immense.

My Power Animal and I had no trouble at all, going straight to my Teacher and finding my Spirit Mate there. But I was stunned who it was. The man standing before me as my Spirit Mate was Jesus. I screamed, "No!" I was confused and not wanting it to be this person/deity/mythic figure. Initially I tried to 'force' the journey to mean something other than the obvious—that I had met this person on my way to meet the "real" Spirit Mate; that this was a "first form" and it would be changing into the "real" Spirit Mate; that discussion during the workshop influenced me and this manifestation was not the work of Spirit. I tried to sit down with Jesus to discuss it, but could not be fully there. I tried to flee. My Teacher then said something (unremembered) that made me recall Michael Harner's words about encountering one's Power Animal: "You take whoever has come. This isn't shopping!" Somewhere near the end [of the journey], Jesus and I were running in a field, free and loose and laughing with the delight of playing. Back in the room [after the callback], I was crying and feeling much more scared than playful. Dana had talked about taking on the qualities of the Spirit Mate and embodying them, and ultimately I knew what my problem was: Equality with Jesus! If Jesus was to be my consort, was I willing to be the Goddess? Was I willing to step into my Power? Gulp! [It took me 13 years to learn on my own what Jesus told me so simply... Discovering my Spirit Mate ultimately forced me to confront myself, own my responsibility and claim my Power.] —S.B.

Inspiration is a gift of the Spirit Mate. I (Shana) have my own tale to tell in this regard. As I was writing the section of this book dealing with the Chukchi, I found that I was bothered by the ultimatum, "Marry me or die." This seemed like a terrible choice and smacked of an 'agenda' and perhaps 'possession'. I felt that I needed to understand "marry me or die" in a more refined way, and asked my own Spirit Mate for help. The following was the result of putting our heads together.

Marriage to a Spirit Mate is a commitment to working together to evolve. The Beloved Other helps strengthen our resolve to speak our truth as part of this evolution. It is easier to keep a promise to him than to myself. When the Spirit Mate says "marry me or die," it is not a threat but rather an offer of redemption. Without the ultimatum, we could languish and perish for our timidity—unworthiness, or other "reasons" we might formulate—and never step forward to begin a deeper quest. Spirit Mates do not tolerate excuses, because they know we are made of sterner stuff and must give this stuff expression. It is not the expressing that will kill us, though we often think so, but rather the holding back that can be our undoing.

The gifts and talents of the shamans are needed by the community. At the macro level, holding the gift back—the reluctant shaman—deprives the community of healing and compassion, of intercourse with the spirit world. On the personal level, holding back is a little death, a denial of one's true self. How many times a day do we kill off a piece of ourselves to avoid responsibility, embarrassment, or out of fear? Holding back is to say "no" to life. In saying "yes" to life and "yes" to the Spirit Mate, we agree to embrace the fullness of existence and to offer a compassionate and loving heart to our community. As the *Course In Miracles* tells us, to give is to receive, and the thing that we think will kill us can make us whole and fully alive. So it isn't that the Spirit Mate will kill us if we don't accept the marriage, but rather we will "kill" ourselves if we don't commit to going forward.

After having this perception crystallize through the inspiration of my Spirit Mate, I came across a confirmation of this reasoning. In a footnote discussing the aggressive aspect of the dakini, Tsultrim Allione remarks that this kind of impersonal force can "...[force] a transformation which might seem negative from the point of view of the rational consciousness...but it brings forth a greater vision and bliss..."[2] Tracking the Beatles, we get by with a little help from our friends.

In what other ways has the Spirit Mate been experienced?

I did a project this year journeying on the Runes, two at a time. He [the Spirit Mate] stepped forward to be my guide. He didn't actually tell me about the Runes, but he accompanied me and would help me remember what I was finding out. If I start to use Runes for others, he will probably be involved. —L.V.

My Spirit Mate has been one of my Teachers since our first meeting. But this relationship has changed a bit. During one journey, I went to see my Spirit Mate at his house...only to find a group of village Elders and others there. Seems I was getting married that night to my Spirit Mate. The ceremony was quite different and very beautiful. Even though we are married, my Spirit Mate has continued to be one of my Teachers. He loves to drum and has taught me a lot about drumming. —Anonymous

When I journey, he is always there with my Wolf to greet me. He is powerful and a weather communicator, and I have called upon him several times to make weather good for me for important events. He has never failed me. Additionally, when holding healings or drum and journey circles, if I get tired, he will aid me and even has 'taken over' drumming for me. He has repeatedly reminded me that his wedding gift to me was an offer to teach me how to talk to the Weather Spirits and work with them to change the weather. He also gives me courage, as he is always standing just behind me and to the left when I need strength. —K.D.

She has clamped down on Ordinary Reality relationships that were not meant to go further. She supported Ordinary Reality relationships that needed encouragement and support. —Shadi

I lean on her heavily when I am in distress about mortal events and she provides me with guidance and spiritual comfort. I believe she also guides me in helping mortals with their problems in life by creating the relationships and helping me help. —Anonymous

He encourages me to spend more time with him in his mountain lands. But he is lighthearted about it, and he makes it clear that it would be for my benefit and enjoyment as well as his. He tells me often how much he loves and admires everything about me. There is nothing that I need to do to secure his continuing love and protection for me; it is freely given and always available. My experience has been very different from the stories from other cultures...there has been nothing coercive about our relationship. —Anonymous

There is great potential in working with a Spirit Mate. The limited exposure that shamanic practitioners have had to this work has demonstrated that for those who are committed to their own growth, the Spirit Mate is a tremendous companion and often a powerful Teacher. There are further avenues to pursue: masculine-feminine balancing, evolution to the Anthropos, and the birth of creative acts in ordinary reality.

It is with great gratitude that we have been able to share the above participant comments in this book. In the workshops, we sit in a circle to remind us that we are all equals, and we are grateful to our students and the spirits for sharing their wisdom with us.

Epilogue

Song for the Spirit Mate — *from the author's journal November 2011(SR)*

Give over, give over
get me out of love's way.
Love has its own pace,
rushing like a river, slow like a breeze.
Give over, give over
get me out of love's way.

Let me greet each day
with newborn eyes
fashioned from the crystal waters of your love.
Wash all I see in your light
that burns out from my heart.
Give over, give over
get me out of love's way.

Let me see your face
in the smiles and the frowns of all I meet.
Words of pain or joy, anger or delight,
transformed by your caress,
fall on me like a lover's touch.
Give over, give over
get me out of love's way.

Let me put down my judgments.
If only for a moment, free me from my fears
arising from my ill-informed separation from you.
Pull me back with the fierceness of your embrace
to your loving truth.
Give over, give over
get me out of love's way.

Notes

Introduction

1. Andrew Harvey and Eryk Hanut, *Perfume of the Desert, Inspirations from Sufi Wisdom*, Quest Books, Wheaton, 1999, p. 109.

2. Brad Edmondson, "All the Lonely People," *AARP: The Magazine*, November/December 2010, p. 54. Loneliness has increased from 20% to 35% in America in the past decade.

3. Ibid., p. 55.
    It doesn't seem that we are any happier or experience more love than we did before our 24/7 ability to email, text and otherwise fill the ethers. In fact, respondents to a survey about loneliness were more likely to agree with the statement, "I have fewer deeper connections now that I keep in touch with people using the Internet."

4. Lowell John Bean, "Power and its Applications in Native California," *Journal of California Anthropology*, Vol. 2, No. 1, Summer 1975, p. 26. Power is a quality distributed throughout the universe. The shaman is known as a power broker, someone who can use it for good or bad ends. The California Indians prior to European contact understood power to have awareness and possess volition. Also, power was seen as a primary agent of movement in the universe. These two characteristics of power, as the California Indians understood them, equate to the immediate definition of power = intelligence + energy. The path of the healer, however, expands to explicitly incorporate love and ethics in the definition, revealing a directed compassion. In calling it directed compassion, we are attempting to highlight a particular value placed on the healer who follows rules for appropriately interacting with power, and respects the channels through which it flows.

5. Carlos Castaneda, *The Teachings of Don Juan: A Yaqui Way of Knowledge*, Pocket Books, New York, 1975, pp. 209-210.
    The words "nonordinary" and "ordinary" reality were introduced in the

works of Carlos Castaneda. They have crept into the parlance of many shamanic practitioners to make the distinction between objective, consensus reality—hence ordinary reality, which occurs when we are in a waking state—versus a reality which is perceived while we are in an altered state of consciousness often used for the shamanic journey. Michael Harner has called this altered state achieved via monotonous percussion the Shamanic State of Consciousness (SSC). See Michael Harner, *The Way of the Shaman,* Harper & Row Publishers, San Francisco, 1990, p. xix.

6. Sandra Harner, "Shamanism and Creativity," *Shamanism,* Vol. 12, No. 2, Fall/Winter 1999, p. 24.

7. Ibid., p. 24.

8. Julia Cameron, *The Artist's Way: A Spiritual Path to Higher Creativity,* Jeremy P. Tarcher/Putnam, New York, 1992, p. 3.

9. In teaching this material, it became apparent that some distinctions were necessary, mostly to highlight what the Spirit Mate is not. Because it is a 'spirit' mate, the being is not a 'soul' mate or Twin Flame. The latter relationships are with living, breathing, embodied ordinary-reality people. A soul mate, according to ancient wisdom traditions, is a person who was created in one's soul group and with whom one has shared many different lifetimes in many different roles. These roles could be anything from family member to dire enemy and were forged to help one learn lessons and transmute karma. A Twin Flame is a highly specialized soul mate, a very rare discovery, and shares one's soul frequency while separate and whole. Esoteric tradition informs us that the reunion of Twin Flames in ordinary reality is generally for higher service and purpose. Also, while the Spirit Mate can be an intimate companion, it is not a spirit who imposes his or her will upon the human partner. A spirit who is within the sphere of a human and exerts influence over him is said to be an obsessing or possessing spirit. More about this in Chapter Six. The Spirit Mate is a compassionate, helping spirit; the human has the ability to exert free will. Extra-terrestrials who engage in non-consensual sexual behavior and experiment with humans are not Spirit Mates. For additional reading on extra-terrestrials and other non-humans consult Baldwin, Modi, Fiore and Rojcewicz.

Chapter 1   Art as Life

1. Philip L. Ravenhill, *Dreams and Reveries: Images of Otherworld Mates among the Baule, West Africa*, Smithsonian Institute Press, Washington and London, 1996, p. 88.

2. Ibid., pp. 2-5.

3. Ibid., p. 43.

4. Ibid., pp. 6-7.

5. Ibid., pp. 60-61.

6. Ibid., p. 35.

7. Marc Ian Barasch, *Healing Dreams: Exploring the Dreams That Can Transform Your Life*, Riverhead Books, New York, 2000, p. 83.

8. Ravenhill, 1996, p. 3.

9. Ibid., p. 16.

10. Philip L. Ravenhill, *The Self and the Other: Personhood and Images among the Baule, Côte d'Ivoire*, Monograph Series No. 28, Los Angeles, 1994, p. 23.

11. Ravenhill, 1996, p. 32.

12. Ravenhill, 1994, p. 24. The diviner, called a wunnzueyifwɛ, is a "revealer of causes."

13. Ravenhill, 1996, p. 6.
    The mouse oracle, a form of myomancy (reading based on the movements of mice), is used by the diviner and consists of two stacked pots connected by a hole. The top pot contains floured sticks (rice chaff) that attract the attention of the mouse in the bottom pot. The mouse moves to the top pot, messes about for a while and then is removed so that the patterns of the sticks as created by the mouse can be read by the diviner. (Ravenhill, 1994, p. 24)

14. Ibid., p. 7.

From the Workshop Journal — #1

1. See Taisha Abelar, *The Sorcerer's Crossing* for details.

2. Se Eliade's *Shamanism* for multiple references to traditional causes of soul loss and methods of recovery. Also, Sandra Ingerman, *Soul Retrieval: Mending the Fragmented Self* and Ai Gvhdi Waya, *Soul Recovery and Extraction* for further discussion. Also, see Caitlín Matthews, *Psychic Shield* for responsible personal conduct.

Chapter 2   The World of Myth

1. Joseph Campbell with Bill Moyers, *The Power of Myth*, Doubleday, New York, 1988, p. xvii.

2. Caitlín Matthews, *Psychic Shield: The Personal Handbook of Psychic Protection*, Ulysses Press, Berkeley, 2006, p. 140.

3. Plato, *The Dialogues of Plato*, J. D. Kaplan, Ed., Washington Square Press, Inc., New York, 1963, p. 20.

4. Campbell, p. xv.
   Bill Moyers, in his foreword, emphasizes that self-aggrandizement is out of place for a hero. This is also true of the shaman, who operates as the 'hollow bone'.

5. Ralph Metzner, *The Well of Remembrance: Rediscovering the Earth Wisdom of Myths of Northern Europe*, Shambhala Publications, Inc., Boston & London, 1994, p. 80.

6. W. Y. Evans-Wentz, *The Fairy Faith in Celtic Countries*, Citadel Press, New York, 1994, p. 79.

7. Samain is the spelling of Samhain used in the Evans-Wentz text. This is November Eve, All Hallows, Halloween.

8. Evans-Wentz, pp. 287-289.

9. Caitlín Matthews, *In Search of Woman's Passionate Soul: Revealing the Daimon Lover Within*, Element, Rockport, 1997, pp. 133-147.

Chapter 3   Saints & Lovers

1. G. Rattray Taylor, *Sex in History*, The Vanguard Press, NY, 1954, p. 42.
   This response was accompanied by the placement of a ring on the candidate's finger and further language that urged the new nun to "forget there all the world, and there be entirely out of the body; there in glowing love embrace your beloved (Saviour) who is come down from heaven into your breast's bower, and hold Him fast until He shall have granted whatsoever you wish for." In keeping with the theme of marriage, the nun's family forfeited to the Church money saved for her dowry.

2. *Webster's Seventh New Collegiate Dictionary*, G. & C. Merriam Company, Springfield, 1970, p. 245.

3. Ibid., p. 883.

4. James H. Leuba, *The Psychology of Religious Mysticism*, Harcourt, Brace & Company, Inc., New York, 1925, p. 101.

5. Ibid., p. 100.
6. Ibid., p. 103.
7. Ibid., p. 103.
8. Ibid., p. 144.
9. Ibid., p. 144.
10. Ibid., p. 61.
11. Ibid., p. 61.
12. Ibid., p. 61.
13. Ibid., p. 63.
14. Ibid., p. 110.
15. Ibid., p. 111.
16. Ibid., pp. 111-112.
17. Ibid., pp. 113-114.
18. Robert Ullman and Judyth Reichenberg-Ullman, *Mystics, Masters, Saints and Sages: Stories of Enlightenment*, Conari Press, Berkeley, 2001, p. 63.
19. Ibid., pp. 67-68. Translation by Judyth Reichenberg-Ullman.
20. Rodney Stark, "A Taxonomy of Religious Experience," *Journal for the Scientific Study of Religion*, Vol. 5, Issue 1, Autumn 1965, p. 105.
21. Leuba, p. 202.
22. Ibid., pp. 116-117.
23. Ibid., p. 202.
24. Ullman, p. 47.
25. Ibid., p. 48.
26. Ibid., p. 48.
27. Ibid., p. 52.
28. Mircea Eliade, *Yoga, Immortality and Freedom*, trans., Willard R. Trask, Princeton University Press, Princeton, 2009, p. 340.

From the Workshop Journal — #3

1. For more insights into the Spiritists, consult Allan Kardec, *The Spirits' Book*, Brotherhood of Life Publishing, Las Vegas, 1989.
2. For further discussion on the nature of helping spirits or Advocates, consult Caitlín Matthews, *Psychic Shield,* pp. 24-25, and various discussions by William Baldwin in *Healing Lost Souls* and *Spirit Releasement Therapy.*

Chapter 4   Divine Election & the Imaginal Realm

1. L. Ia. Shternberg, "Shamanism and Religious Election," *Introduction to Soviet Ethnography*, Vol. 1, Stephen P. Dunn and Ethel Dunn, Eds., Highgate Road Social Science Research Station, Berkeley, 1974, p. 74.

2. Mircea Eliade, *Shamanism: Archaic Techniques of Ecstasy*, trans. Willard R. Trask, Princeton University Press, 1964, pp. 173, 259.

3. The Norse model of the Tree of Worlds is a bit more complicated. It includes Midgard, or the Human World of Ordinary Reality at the center. Above it on the axis are Ljossalheim, the Realm of Light and the Elves, and above that, Asgard, Garden of the Sky-gods. Below Midgard on the axis are Svartalfheim, the Realm of the Black Elves, Stone Spirits and Dwarves, and below that, Hel, the Underworld of the Death Goddess Hel. There are two other axes included in the model: north-south and east-west. To the north is Niflheim, the Realm of Ice and Cold. To the south is Muspellheim, the Realm of Fire and Heat. To the east is Jötunheim, the Realm of the Giants. And, to the west is Vanaheim, the Realm of Land and Sea-Deities. See Ralph Metzner's *The Well of Remembrance* p. 201 for a diagram.

4. Henri Corbin, "Mundus Imaginalis, or the Imaginary and the Imaginal," p. 1, http://hermetic.com/bey/mundus_imaginal.html, last accessed 1/2/11.

5. Ibid, p. 1.

6. Ibid, p. 8.

7. For more information on percussion and the brain, see Andrew Neher, "A Physiological Explanation of Unusual Behavior in Ceremonies Involving Drums," *Human Biology*, Vol. 34, May 1962, pp. 151-160, and Barbara W. Lex, "The Neurobiology of Ritual Trance," *The Spectrum of Ritual: A Biogenetic Structural Analysis,* Eugene G. d'Aquili, Columbia University Press, New York, 1979, pp. 117-151.

8. Valentina Gorbatcheva and Marina Federova, *The Peoples of the Great North: Art and Civilization of Siberia*, Parkstone Press, New York, 2000. This is a lovely book with glossy photos capturing the people and landscape of Siberia.

9. Eliade, 1964, p. 77.

10. Shternberg, p. 74.

11. Ibid., pp. 73-74.

12. Ibid., p. 75.

13. Ibid., p. 75.

14. Ibid., p. 76.

15. William Madsen, "Shamanism in Mexico," *Southwestern Journal of Anthropology*, Vol. 11, 1955, pp. 48-57.

From the Workshop Journal — #4

1. Waldemar Bogoras, "The Chuckchee – Religion," *Memoirs of the American Museum of Natural History*, Volume XI, Leiden, E.J. Brill Ltd., New York, 1904, p. 281. (Chuckchee can also be spelled Chukchi.)

Chapter 5   Gender & the Call

1. The Three Initiates, *The Kybalion: A Study of Hermetic Philosophy of Ancient Egypt and Greece*, The Yogi Publication Society, Chicago, 1940, pp. 25-26.
   The principles are: I. The Principle of Mentalism; II. The Principle of Correspondence; III. The Principle of Vibration; IV. The Principle of Polarity; V. The Principle of Rhythm; VI. The Principle of Cause and Effect; and VII. The Principle of Gender.

2. Ibid., p. 183.

3. Ibid., pp. 183-184.

4. Marjorie Mandelstam Balzar, "Sacred Genders in Siberia: Shamans, bear festivals and androgyny," *Gender Reversals and Gender Cultures*, Sabrina Petra Ramet, Ed., Routledge, London & New York, 1996, p. 164.

5. It is interesting to note the distinction between *healing* and *curing*. A discussion of this appears in *Boiling Energy* by Richard Katz. For the Kalahari Kung people, *cure* is that someone gets better; there is an alleviation of symptoms. *Healing* seeks to correct an imbalance in the universe; that balance may actually be reestablished as a relief of symptoms or the patient's death (pp. 53-54).

6. Sabrina Petra Ramet, "Gender Reversals and Gender Cultures: An Introduction," in *Gender Reversals and Gender Cultures*, p. 2.

7. Sabine Lang, "There is More Than Just Women and Men: Gender Variance in North American Indian Cultures," in *Gender Reversals and Gender Cultures*, p. 185.

8. Ibid., p. 184.

9. Anne Bolin, "Traversing Gender," in *Gender Reversals and Gender Cultures*, p. 22.

10. Lang, p. 193, Balzar, p. 165.

11. Ramet, p. 4.

12. Ibid., p. 4.

13. Ibid., p. 5.

14. Balzar, p. 167.

15. Shternberg, p. 77.

16. Balzar, p. 167.

17. Ibid., p. 167.

18. Ana Mariella Bacigalupo, *Shamans of the Foye Tree: Gender, Power, and Healing Among the Chilean Mapuche,* University of Texas Press, Austin, 2007. Chapter 4 for this entire section.

19. Ibid., p. 89.

20. Ibid., p. 92.

Chapter 6   Inspirational Possession

1. Erika Bourguignon, *Possession,* Chandler & Sharp Publishers, Inc., San Francisco, 1976, p. 10.

2. Masao Maki, *In Search of Brazil's Quantum Surgeon: The Dr. Fritz Phenomenon,* Cadence Books, San Francisco, 1997, pp. 48, 67.

3. M. Lewis, *Ecstatic Religion: A Study of Shamanism and Spirit Possession, Third Edition,* Routledge, London & New York, 2003, pp. 101, 105.

4. Robert F. Bailey and Irene Lo, "The Spirit Wife of Myanmar," *Shamanism,* Fall/Winter 2002, Vol. 15, No. 2, p. 34.

5. When a practitioner goes to the spirits in the Upper and Lower Worlds or to the non-ordinary aspect of the Middle World for information using an altered state of consciousness, it is known as a journey. When the spirits come to the practitioner in the Middle World, it is often called mediumship or channeling.

6. Verrier Elwin, *The Religion of an Indian Tribe,* Oxford University Press, London, 1955, p. 470 – 471.

7. Ibid., pp. 158-163.

8. Ibid., p. 471.

9. Ibid., p. 135.

10. Ibid., p. 136.

11. The Saorans also install spirits in ikons, ceremonially created paintings, on the walls of houses. Made according to the instructions of specific spirits, given in dream to the artist, the ikon becomes the two dimensional home for the spirit, and the place where officially-induced trances occur. Ikons are painted for tutelaries. See Elwin, pp. 147, 401-405, 470.

12. Elwin, p. 136.

13. Ibid., p. 137

14. Ibid., p. 168.

15. Ibid., p. 170.

16. The Kuranmaran are a kind of male Saoran functionary. They have a tutelary wife in the Under World who assists and guides them. They diagnose and cure disease and can offer sacrifices though they do not do the killing themselves. See Elwin, *The Religion of an Indian Tribe,* Chapters Four and Five for additional functionaries and details.

17. Elwin, 470.

18. Ibid., p. 68.

19. Ibid., p. 477.

20. Ibid., pp. 476-477.

21. Ibid., p. 148.

22. Melford E. Spiro, *Burmese Supernaturalism,* Prentice-Hall, Inc., Englewood Cliffs, 1967, p. 243.

23. Ibid., p. 209.

24. Bailey and Lo, p. 33. In this article the transliteration of *nat kadaw* is *natgadaw.*

25. Ibid., p. 33.

26. Spiro, p. 205.

27. Bailey and Lo, p. 31.

28. Spiro, pp. 216-218.

29. For a full discussion of the debate consult: G. W. Domhoff, *Senoi Dream Theory: Myth, Scientific Method, and the Dreamwork Movement, March 2003.* Retrieved from the World Wide Web: http://dreamresearch.net/Library/senoi.html Last accessed 10/22/2011.

30. Marina Roseman, *Healing Sounds from the Malaysian Rainforest: Temiar Music and Medicine,* University of California Press, Berkeley, 1991, p. 25.

31. Ibid., p. 53.

32. Ibid., p. 72.

33. Ibid., pp. 30, 116.

34. Ibid., p. 115.

35. Ibid., p. 123.

36. Ibid., p. 152-153.

37. Ibid., p. 153.

38. Ibid., p. 107.

39. Ibid., p. 164.

40. Ibid., p. 158.

41. For differing perspectives on the definition of the word shaman and how it should be applied, consult William Lebra and Alice B. Kehoe. Lebra's working definition recognizes shamans as interacting with supernatural powers in socially acceptable ways and having the ability to enter into trance states at will (cited in Laurel Kendall, 1987). Kehoe is adamant that the word *shaman* belongs solely to Siberia.

42. According to Spiro, the few male *nat kadaws* seem to be latent or manifest homosexual, transvestite, or effeminate, and their nat spouse is always female. Dressing as her for dancing, the male *nat kadaw* becomes the female spouse and acts out the feminine components of his personality. Likewise, Spiro goes on to report that many female practitioners are highly masculine in manner and may satisfy masculine attributes through the identification with the nat husband. See Spiro, p. 220.

From the Workshop Journal — #6

1. Leuba, p. 1.

2. Stark, pp. 112-115.

3. To be clear, not every culture holds a belief in an Absolute, Supreme Being or Creator. A great example of such a culture is the Pirahã of the Amazonian jungle. See Daniel L. Everett, *Don't Sleep There Are Snakes*, Pantheon Books, New York, 2008.

4. Jean-Yves Leloup, *Being Still: Reflections on an Ancient Mystical Tradition*, Paulist Press, New York/Mahwah, 2003, p. 94.

Chapter 7   Mysticism, Ecstasy & the Anthropos

1. Bernard McGinn, "Mystical Union in Judaism, Christianity, and Islam," *Encyclopedia of Religion, Second Edition*, Vol. 9, Lindsay Jones Ed., Macmillan Reference USA, Detroit, 2005, p. 6334.

2. Arvind Sharma, "Ecstasy," in *Encyclopedia of Religion*, Second Edition, Vol. 4, p. 2680.

3. McGinn, p. 6335.

4. Ibid., p. 6335.

5. Eliade, 1964, pp. 509-510.

6. See footnote 4 in the Introduction.

7. Stephen Harrod Buhner, *The Secret Teachings of Plants*, Bear & Co., Rochester, 2004, Chapter Five. See also Gershon Winkler, *Magic of the Ordinary: Recovering the Shamanic in Judaism*, North Atlantic Books, Berkeley, 2003, pp. 117-120, for a somewhat similar perspective.

8. Sharma, p. 2678.

9. Ibid., p. 2679.

10. Ibid., p. 2680.

11. Daniel C. Matt, *Zohar: Annotated & Explained*, Skylight Paths Publishing, Woodstock, 2002, p. xxi-xxiv.

12. Ibid., p. xxiii.

13. The cosmic tree and World Tree are often called the *axis mundi* or Axis of the World. This axis is thought to pass through the center of the world, thus allowing the shaman to make his ascent into the sky. See Mircea Eliade, *The Sacred and the Profane, The Nature of Religion*, trans. Willard R. Trask, Harcourt, Brace & World, Inc., New York, 1959, Chapter One, for a complete discussion.

14. Eliade, 1964, p. 169.

15. Matt, p. xvi.

16. Ibid., p. xxvi.

17. Ibid., p. xxvii.

18. Ibid., p. xiv.

19. Ibid., p. xxvii.

20. Ibid., p. xxviii.

21. Jean-Yves Leloup, *The Gospel of Mary Magdalene*, Inner Traditions, Rochester, 2002, pp. 5-6.

22. Jean-Yves Leloup, *The Gospel of Philip*, Inner Traditions, Rochester, 2004, pp. 1-3.
   Currently, the four canonical gospels of the Church are those of Matthew, Mark, Luke and John. One gospel, the Gospel of Peter, was considered canonical until 180 C.E. when the Muratori Canon judged that it was not acceptable. However, it was considered to be canonical into the third century by some Syrian churches.

23. Ibid., p. 102.

24. Ibid., p. 13.

25. Ibid., p. 18.

26. See footnote 5, Introduction.

27. Leloup, 2004, p. 83.

28. Ibid., 2004, pp. 28-29.

29. Ibid., 2004, p. 107.

30. Ibid., 2004, p. 24.

From the Workshop Journal — #7

1. Tsultrim Allione, *Women of Wisdom*, Snow Lion Publications, Ithaca, 2000, p. 217, n. 109.

2. Jean-Yves Leloup, *Being Still: Reflections on an Ancient Mystical Tradition*, Paulist Press, New York/Mahwah, 2003, pp. 2-12.

Reel Life: Spirit Mates in Popular Culture — #1

1. For full lyrics, go to http://www.bobbydarin.net/dreamlyrics.html. Lyrics transcribed by Marilyn Brown and Jane Penny. Last accessed 6/10/11.

2. For full lyrics see http://www.stlyrics.com/lyrics/ridingincarswithboys/dream.htm. Last accessed 6/10/11.

Chapter 8   Dreamers & Daimons

1. Our use of the word "contrasexual other" tracks Caitlín Matthews, who uses it to signify the opposite sex Other in heterosexuals. For homosexuals, this Other may be of the same sex. (Matthews, 1997, p. 233)

2. This is the same Asklepius of Chapter 1, just a different transliteration.

3. Fred Alan Wolf, *The Dreaming Universe*, Simon & Schuster, New York, 1994.

4. Robert Moss, *Dreaming True*, Pocket Books, New York, 2000, pp. 129-130.

5. Ibid., p. 129.

6. Michael Harner, "A Core Shamanic Theory of Dreams," *Shamanism*, December 2010, Issue 23, pp. 2-4.

7. David Cloutier, "Things a Shaman Sees," *Spirit, Spirit: Shaman Songs*, Copper Beech Press, Providence, 1980, p. 35–36.

This line comes from a version of a Chuckchee shaman's song and is an adaptation of the original which appeared in Bogoras' book *The Chuckchee—Religion.*

8. Harner, p. 3.

9. Stephen Aizenstat, Ph. D., *Dream Tending*, Spring Journal, Inc., New Orleans, 2009, pp. 109-110.

10. Ibid., p. 117.

11. Ibid., pp. 117-118.

12. Ibid., p. 124.

13. Ibid., p. 125.

14. Ibid., p. 127.

15. Carl Jung, "Aion: Phenomenology of the Self (The Ego, the Shadow, the Syzygy: Anima/Animus)," *The Portable Jung*, Joseph Campbell, Ed., R. F. C. Hull, Trans., Penguin Books, 1971, p. 151.

16. Ibid., p. 153.

17. Ibid., p. 154.

18. Some may comment that this strikes a false dichotomy. The shaman as spirit worker was the first psychologist.

19. Matthews, 1997, p. 2.

20. Patrick Harpur, *Daimonic Reality: Understanding Otherworld Encounters*, Penguin Books, New York, 1994, p. 54.

21. Ibid., p. 40.

22. Ibid., p. 55.

23. Ibid., p. 55.

24. Ibid., p. 56.

25. Ibid., p. 56.

26. Ibid., p. 61.

27. Ibid., p. 69.

28. Matthews, 1997, p. 7.

29. While the opposite sex Other typically exists for heterosexuals, a lesbian is more likely to have a female inner beloved, and a gay man a male inner beloved.

30. Ibid., pp. 21-22.

31. Ibid., p. 20.

32. Caitlín Matthews, *Sophia: Goddess of Wisdom, Bride of God*, Quest Books, Wheaton, 2001, p. 7.

33. Matthews, 1997, p. 223.

From the Workshop Journal — #8

1. Anthony Louis, *Tarot, Plain and Simple*, Llewellyn Publications, St. Paul, 2000, p. 3.
2. Ibid., p. 117.
3. Ibid., p. 247. The querent is the person asking questions of the Tarot.

Chapter 9   Dakas & Dakinis

1. Keith Dowman, *Sky Dancer: The Secret Life and Songs of the Lady Yeshe Tsogyel*, Snow Lion Publications, Ithaca, 1996, p. 86.
2. Mircea Eliade emphasizes "the structural difference that distinguishes classic Yoga from Shamanism. Although the latter is not without certain techniques of concentration…its final goal is always ecstasy and the soul's ecstatic journey through the various cosmic regions, whereas Yoga pursues enstasis, final concentration of the spirit and 'escape' from the cosmos." See Eliade, 1964, p. 417.
3. Eliade, 2009, pp. 4-5.
4. Ibid., p. 200.
5. Ibid., p. 254.
6. Ibid., p. 254.
7. Shternberg, p. 81.
8. Ibid., p. 80.
9. Matthews, 1997, p. 37.
10. Allione, p. 116.
11. Dowman, p. 230.
12. Ibid., p. 221.
13. Allione, pp. 286-287, n. 67.
14. Dowman, p. 229.
15. Allione, pp. 288-289, n. 80.
16. Dowman, p. 231.
17. Allione, pp. 288-289, n. 80.
18. Ibid., pp. 288-289, n. 80.
19. Dowman, p. 235.
20. Allione, pp. 288-289, n. 80.
21. Ibid., p. 91.
22. Dowman, p. 241.
23. The word *dakini* has many shades of meaning. When capitalized, if often refers to Yeshe Tsogyel as the Consort of the Guru

Padmasambhava. In small case, it can refer to a myriad of beings known to the Tibetans as the *khandroma*, or "Sky-Walkers." The *dakini* is feminine, active, at once a spiritual principle and a female sexual partner. (Dowman, p. 273).

24. Dowman, p. x.
25. The *kayas* or 'bodies of the Buddha' may be understood as fields of perception. The Nirmanakaya is the dimension closest to us in perception and is the dimension of form and manifestation associated with physicality. This is the only *kaya* that can be perceived by normal humans. With initiations and empowerments, some can perceive the Sambhogakaya, the dimension of radiant energy and light which is beyond dualistic limitations. The dimension of emptiness and unconditioned truth is the Dharmakaya which contains the potential for everything.
26. Ibid., p. 36.
27. Ibid., p. 37.
28. Ibid., p. 194, n 25.
29. Ibid., p. 38.
30. Ibid., p. 39-40.
31. Ibid., p. 44.
32. Matthews, 2001, p. 365.
33. Dowman, p. 224.
34. Allione, p. 110.
35. Ibid., p. 112.
36. Dowman, p. 60.

Chapter 10   Modern Martyr

1. Vere Chappell, *Sexual Outlaw, Erotic Mystic, The Essential Ida Craddock*, Weiser Books, San Francisco, 2010, p. 27.
2. Ibid., p. 175.
3. Ibid., p. 3.
4. Ibid., p. 3, n. 13.
5. Ibid., p. xviii-xix.
6. Ibid., p. 3.
7. The World's Fair was the shortened name for what was officially called the Columbian Exposition. The fair featured living exhibits such as the Enutseak family, Inuits from Labrador. When the family wasn't living

at the fair, they wintered at Coney Island in New York. See James Ring Adams, "The Sideshow Olympics: Weirdness and Racism at St. Louis, 1904," *American Indian*, Summer, 2012, pp. 18-21.

8. Chappell, p. 5.
9. Ibid., p. 11.
10. Ibid., p. 20.
11. Ibid., p. 26.
12. Ibid., p. 33.
13. Ibid., p. 41.
14. Ibid., p. 141.
15. Eliade, 2009, pp. 406-407.
16. Chappell, p. 141. Compare/contrast to Aizenstat's Third Body.
17. Ibid., 145.
18. Ibid., 219.
19. Ibid., 245.
20. Allione, pp. 284-285, n. 48.

From the Workshop Journal — #10

1. Allione, p. 104.
2. Khenchen Palden Sherab Rinpoche and Khenpo Tsewang Dongyal Rinpoche, *The Dark Red Amulet*, Snow Lion Publications, Ithaca, 2008, p. 80.
3. See http://deadlysins.com/virtues.html. Last accessed 6/14/12.
4. Samuel Sagan, *Entity Possession, Freeing the Energy Body of Negative Influences*, Destiny Books, Rochester, 1997, p. 34.
5. See http://deadlysins.com/virtues.html. Last accessed 6/14/12.

From the Workshop Journal — #11

1. Eric Weiner attempts to answer this question in his book *The Geography of Bliss*. One of his conclusions is that happiness is 100% relational (see pp. 75, 324-325).
2. http://www.usnews.com/science/articles/2011/03/03/happiness-improves-health-and-lengthens-life. Last accessed 6/19/12.
3. Check out the library at http://www.gratefulness.org.

Chapter 11   The Experience

1. Student experiences are very personal and we respect the right to privacy. Therefore, in certain cases, we have credited "Anonymous" to various reports. Students were somewhat hesitant to reply to questionnaires after engaging in this work. We hope that greater openness and acceptance of this work will allow others to step forward with comments in the future.

2. Allione, p. 208, n. 24.

Bibliography

Abelar, Taisha, *The Sorcerer's Crossing*, Penguin Books, New York, 1992.

Adams, James Ring, "The Sideshow Olympics: Weirdness and Racism at St. Louis, 1904," *American Indian*, Summer 2012.

Aizenstat, Stephen, *Dream Tending*, Spring Journal, Inc., New Orleans, 2009.

Allione, Tsultrim, *Women of Wisdom*, Snow Lion Publications, Ithaca, 2000.

Bacigalupo, Ana Mariella, *Shamans of the Foye Tree: Gender, Power, and Healing Among the Chilean Mapuche*, University of Texas Press, Austin, 2007.

Bailey, Robert F. and Irene Lo, "The Spirit Wife of Myanmar," *Shamanism*, Vol. 15, No. 1, Fall/Winter 2002.

Baldwin, William, *Healing Lost Souls: Releasing Unwanted Spirits from Your Energy Body*, Hampton Roads, Charlottesville, 2003.

Baldwin, William, *Spirit Releasement Therapy: A Technique Manual, Second Edition*, Headline Books, Inc., Terra Alta, 2005.

Balzer, Marjorie Mandelstam, "Sacred Genders in Siberia: Shamans, bear festivals, and androgyny," *Gender Reversals and Gender Cultures*, Ed. Sabrina Petra Ramet, Routledge, London & New York, 1996.

Barasch, Marc Ian, *Healing Dreams: Exploring the Dreams That Can Transform Your Life*, Riverhead Books, New York, 2000.

Bean, Lowell John, "Power and its Applications in Native California," *Journal of California Anthropology,* Vol. 2, No. 1, Summer 1975.

Bly, Robert, *Kabir: Ecstatic Poems,* Beacon Press, Boston, 2004.

Bogoras, Waldemar, "The Chuckchee – Religion," *Memoirs of the American Museum of Natural History,* Volume XI, Leiden, E.J. Brill Ltd.; New York, 1904.

Bolin, Anne, "Traversing Gender: Cultural context and gender practices," *Gender Reversals and Gender Cultures,* Ed. Sabrina Petra Ramet, Routledge, London & New York, 1996.

Bourguignon, Erika, *Possession,* Chandler & Sharp Publishers, Inc., San Francisco, 1976.

Buhner, Stephen Harrod, *The Secret Teachings of Plants,* Bear & Company, Rochester, 2004.

Campbell, Joseph and Bill Moyers, *The Power of Myth,* Doubleday, New York, 1988.

Cameron, Julia, *The Artist's Way: A Spiritual Path to Higher Creativity,* Jeremy P. Tarcher/Putnam, New York, 1992.

Castaneda, Carlos, *The Teachings of Don Juan: A Yaqui Way of Knowledge,* Pocket Books, New York, 1975.

Chappell, Vere, *Sexual Outlaw, Erotic Mystic: The Essential Ida Craddock,* Weiser Books, San Francisco, 2010.

Cloutier, David, *Spirit, Spirit: Shaman Songs,* Copper Beech Press, Providence, 1980.

Corbin, Henri, "*Mundus Imaginalis, or the Imaginary and the Imaginal,*" http://hermetic.com/bey/mundus_imaginalis.htm, Web. 2 Jan. 2011.

Culling, Louis T., *Sex Magick: A Classic of Erotic Mysticism,* Llewellyn Publications, St. Paul, 1992.

David-Neel, Alexandra, *Magic and Mystery in Tibet,* Dover Publications, New York, 1971.

Domhoff, G. William, "Senoi Dream Theory: Myth, Scientific Method, and the Dreamwork Movement," March 2003, http://psych.ucsc.edu/dreams/Library/senoi.html, Web. 11 Oct. 2010.

Dowman, Keith, *Sky Dancer: The Secret Life and Songs of the Lady Yeshe Tsogyel,* Snow Lion Publications, Ithaca, 1996.

Edmondson, Brad, "All the Lonely People," *AARP: The Magazine,* November/December 2010.

Eliade, Mircea, *The Sacred and the Profane, The Nature of Religion,* trans. Willard R. Trask, Harcourt, Brace & World, Inc., New York, 1959.

Eliade, Mircea, *Shamanism: Archaic Techniques of Ecstasy,* trans. Willard R. Trask, Princeton University Press, Princeton, 1964.

Eliade, Mircea, *Yoga: Immortality and Freedom,* trans. Willard R. Trask, Princeton University Press, Princeton, 2009.

Elwin, Verrier, *The Religion of an Indian Tribe,* Oxford University Press, Oxford, 1955.

Evans, Cheryl, *The Usborne Book of Greek & Norse Legends,* Usborne Publishing Ltd., Tulsa, 2003.

Evans-Wentz, W. Y., *The Fairy-Faith in Celtic Countries,* Citadel Press, New York, 1994.

Everett, Daniel, L., *Don't Sleep There Are Snakes,* Pantheon Books, New York, 2008.

Fiore, Edith, *Encounters,* Ballantine Books, New York, 1989.

Fiore, Edith, *The Unquiet Dead,* Ballantine Books, New York, 1987.

Gorbatcheva, Valentina and Marina Federova, *The Peoples of the Great North: Art and Civilization of Siberia,* Parkstone Press, New York, 2000.

Guillaumont, A., Henri-Charles Puech, Gilles Quispel, Walter Till, and Yassah 'Abd Al Masih, *The Gospel According to Thomas,* Harper & Row Publishers, New York, 1959.

Harner, Michael, "A Core Shamanic Theory of Dreams," *Shamanism,* Issue 23, December 2010.

Harner, Michael, *The Way of the Shaman*, Harper & Row Publishers, San Francisco, 1990.

Harner, Sandra, "Shamanism and Creativity," *Shamanism*, Vol. 12, No. 2, Fall/Winter 1999.

Harpur, Patrick, *Daimonic Reality: Understanding Otherworld Encounters*, Arkana, London, 1995.

Harvey, Andrew and Eryk Hanut, *Perfume of the Desert: Inspirations from Sufi Wisdom*, Quest Books, Wheaton, 1999.

Ingerman, Sandra, *Soul Retrieval: Mending the Fragmented Self*, HarperSanFrancisco, New York, 1991.

Ireland-Frey, Louise, *Freeing the Captives*, Hampton Roads, Charlottesville, 1999.

Jampolsky, Gerald, *Love is Letting Go of Fear*, Celestial Arts, Milbrae, 1979.

Jung, Karl, "Aion: Phenomenology of the Self (The Ego, the Shadow, the Syzygy: Anima/Animus)," *The Portable Jung*, Joseph Campbell, Ed., R. F. C. Hull, Trans., Penguin Books, New York, 1986.

Kalweit, Holger, *Dreamtime & Inner Space: The World of the Shaman*, trans. Werner Wunsche, Shambhala, Boston, 1988.

Kardec, Allan, *The Spirits' Book*, Brotherhood of Life Publishing, Las Vegas, 1989.

Katz, Richard, *Boiling Energy: Community Healing Among the Kalahari Kung*, Harvard University Press, Cambridge & London, 1982.

Kendall, Laurel, *Shamanism, Housewives, and Other Restless Spirits: Women in Korean Ritual Life*, University of Hawaii Press, Honolulu, 1987.

Krippner, Stanley, "Cross-Cultural Approaches to Multiple Personality Disorder: Practices in Brazilian Spiritism," *Ethos*, Vol. 15, No. 3, September 1987.

Lang, Sabine, "There is More Than Just Women and Men: Gender variance in North American Indian cultures," *Gender Reversals and Gender Cultures,* Ed. Sabrina Petra Ramet, Routledge, London & New York, 1996.

Leloup, Jean-Yves, *Being Still: Reflections on an Ancient Mystical Tradition,* Paulist Press, New York/Mahwah, 2003.

Leloup, Jean-Yves, *The Gospel of Mary Magdalene,* trans. Joseph Rowe, Inner Traditions, Rochester, 2002.

Leloup, Jean-Yves, *The Gospel of Philip,* trans. Joseph Rowe, Inner Traditions, Rochester, 2004.

Leuba, James H., *The Psychology of Religious Mysticism,* Harcourt, Brace & Company, Inc., New York, 1925.

Lewis, I. M., *Ecstatic Religion: a Study of Shamanism and Spirit Possession, Third Edition,* Routledge, New York, 2003.

Lex, Barbara W., "The Neurobiology of Ritual Trance," *The Spectrum of Ritual: A Biogenetic Structural Analysis,* Eugene G. d'Aquili, Charles D. Laughlin, Jr., John McManus, Columbia University Press, New York, 1979.

Madsen, William, "Shamanism in Mexico," *Southwestern Journal of Anthropology,* No. 11, 1955.

Maki, Masao, *In Search of Brazil's Quantum Surgeon: The Dr. Fritz Phenomenon,* Cadence Books, San Francisco, 1998.

Matt, Daniel C., Trans., *Zohar: Annotated & Explained,* Skylight Paths Publishing, Woodstock, 2002.

Matthews, Caitlín, *In Search of Woman's Passionate Soul: Revealing the Daimon Lover Within,* Element, Rockport, 1997.

Matthews, Caitlín, *Psychic Shield: The Personal Handbook of Psychic Protection,* Ulysses Press, Berkeley, 2006.

Matthews, Caitlín, *Sophia: Goddess of Wisdom, Bride of God,* Quest Books, Wheaton, 2001.

McGinn, Bernard, "Mystical Union in Judaism, Christianity, and Islam," *Encyclopedia of Religion,* Ed. Lindsay Jones, 2nd ed. Vol. 9, Detroit: Macmillian Reference USA, 2005. 6334 - 6341. *Gale Virtual Reference Library.* Web. 21 Jan. 2011.

Metzner, Ralph, *The Well of Remembrance: Rediscovering the Earth Wisdom Myths of Northern Europe,* Shambhala Publications, Inc., Boston & London, 1994.

Modi, Shakuntala, *Remarkable Healings: A Psychiatrist Discovers Unsuspected Roots of Mental and Physical Illness,* Hampton Roads Publishing Company, Charlottesville, 1997.

Moss, Robert, *Dreaming True: How to Dream Your Future and Change Your Life for the Better,* Pocket Books, New York, 2000.

Neher, Andrew, "A Physiological Explanation of Unusual Behavior in Ceremonies Involving Drums," *Human Biology,* Vol. 34, May 1962

Nicola, Rev. John J., *Diabolical Possession and Exorcism,* Tan Books and Publishers, Inc., Rockford, 1974.

Palden Sherab, Khenchen and Khenpo Tsewang Dongyal, *The Dark Red Amulet,* Snow Lion Publications, Ithaca, 2008.

Perkins, John, *Shapeshifting: Shamanic Techniques for Global and Personal Transformation,* Destiny Books, Rochester, 1997.

Plato, *The Dialogues of Plato,* J. D. Kaplan, Ed., Washington Square Press, Inc., New York, 1963.

Ramet, Sabrina Petra, "Gender Reversals and Gender Cultures: An introduction," *Gender Reversals and Gender Cultures,* Ed. Sabrina Petra Ramet, Routledge, London & New York, 1996.

Ravenhill, Philip L., *Dreams and Reverie: Images of Otherworld Mates Among the Baule, West Africa,* Smithsonian Institution Press, Washington, 1996.

Ravenhill, Philip L., *The Self and Other: Personhood & Images among the Baule, Cote d'Ivoire,* Monograph Series, No. 28, Los Angeles, 1994.

Rojcewicz, Peter M., "Strange Bedfellows: The Folklore of Other-Sex," *Critique: A Journal Exposing Consensus Reality,* Issue 29, 1989.

Roseman, Marina, *Healing Sounds from the Malaysian Rainforest,* University of California Press, Berkeley, 1991.

Sagan, Samuel, *Entity Possession, Freeing the Energy Body of Negative Influences,* Destiny Books, Rochester, 1997.

Sharma, Arvind, "Ecstacy," *Encyclopedia of Religion,* Ed. Lindsay Jones, 2nd ed. Vol. 4, Detroit: Macmillian Reference USA, 2005. 2677 - 2683. *Gale Virtual Reference Library.* Web. 21 Jan. 2011.

Shternberg, L. Ia., "Shamanism and Religious Election," *Introduction to Soviet Ethnography, Vol. 1,* Stephen P. Dunn and Ethel Dunn, Eds., Highgate Road Social Science Research Station, Berkeley, 1974.

Spiro, Melford E., *Burmese Supernaturalism,* Prentice-Hall, Inc., Englewood Cliffs, 1967.

Stark, Rodney, "A Taxonomy of Religious Experience," *Journal for the Scientific Study of Religion,* Vol. 5, Issue 1, Autumn 1965.

Taylor, G. Rattray, *Sex in History,* The Vanguard Press, New York, 1954.

Three Initiates, *The Kybalion: A Study of Hermetic Philosophy of Ancient Egypt and Greece,* The Yogi Publication Society, Chicago, 1940.

Ullman, Robert and Judyth Reichenberg-Ullman, *Mystics, Masters, Saints and Sages: Stories of Enlightenment,* Conari Press, Berkeley, 2001.

Waya, Ai Gvhdi, *Soul Recovery and Extraction,* Blue Turtle Publishing, Cottonwood, 1993.

Weiner, Eric, *The Geography of Bliss,* Twelve, New York & Boston, 2008.

Welch, J. L., "Cross-Dressing and Cross-Purposes: Gender possibilities in the Acts of Thecla," *Gender Reversals and Gender Cultures,* Ed. Sabrina Petra Ramet, Routledge, London & New York, 1996.

Winkler, Gershon, *Magic of the Ordinary: Recovering the Shamanic in Judaism,* North Atlantic Books, Berkeley, 2003.

Wolf, Fred Alan, *The Dreaming Universe,* Simon & Schuster, New York, 1994.

Filmography

Down to Earth (1947)
    Director: Alexander Hall
    Actors: Rita Hayworth, Larry Parks and Marc Platt
    Writers: Harry Segall (play "Heaven Can Wait"), Edwin Blum
    (screenplay), Don Hartman (screenplay)

Portrait of Jennie (1948)
    Director: William Dieterle
    Actors: Jennifer Jones, Joseph Cotten and Ethel Barrymore
    Writers: Robert Nathan (novel), Leonardo Bercovici
    (adaptation), Paul Osborn (screenplay), Peter Berneis
    (screenplay), Ben Hecht (uncredited), David O. Selznick
    (uncredited)

The Ghost and Mrs. Muir (1947)
    Director: Joseph Mankiewicz
    Actors: Gene Tierney, Rex Harrison and George Sanders
    Writers: Philip Dunne (screenplay), R.A. Dick (novel)

Websites

Bobby Darin Lyrics, http://www.bobbydarin.net/dreamlyrics.html,
    Web. 10 June 2011.
Everly Brothers Lyrics, http://www.stlyrics.com/lyrics/
    ridingincarswithboys/dream.htm, Web. 10 June 2011.
Gratitude, http://www.gratefulness.org/, Web. 14 June 2012.
Happiness, http://www.usnews.com/science/articles/2011/03/03/
    happiness-improves-health-and-lengthens-life, Web. 19 June
    2012.
Seven Deadly Sins and Counterparts, http://deadlysins.com/
    virtues.html, Web. 14 June 2012.

Index

To contact the authors or to schedule a workshop:

Dana Robinson danacougar@goeaston.net
Shana Robinson gbravehearthawks@goeaston.net
www.shamantracks.com

CPSIA information can be obtained at www.ICGtesting.com
Printed in the USA
BVOW061926170413

318452BV00003B/66/P